OAKLAND,
JACK LONDON,
and ME

Also by Eric Miles Williamson

East Bay Grease
Two-Up

Jack London,
and Me

Eric Miles
Williamson

Texas Review Press • Huntsville, Texas

10 9 8 7 6 5 4 3 2 1

Texas Review Press
English Department
Sam Houston State University
Huntsville, Texas 77341-2146

Excerpts from *The Letters of Jack London,* Earle Labor, Robert C. Leitz, III, and I. Milo Shepherd, editors. Copyright © 1988 by the Board of Trustees of the Leland Stanford Jr. University. Reprinted with permission.

Author photo by Eric Lauer. Printed with permission. Front and back photos by James F. Nelson. Printed with permission. Index compiled by Rob Johnson. Cover and interior design by Richard Foerster.

Portions of this book have appeared in *The Virginia Quarterly Review*, *The Chattahoochee Review*, and *American Book Review*.

Library of Congress Cataloging in Publication Data

Williamson, Eric Miles.
  Oakland, Jack London, and me / by Eric Miles Williamson. -- 1st ed.
    p. cm.
  Includes index.
  ISBN-13: 978-1-933896-11-3 (pbk. : alk. paper)
  ISBN-10: 1-933896-11-6 (pbk. : alk. paper)
1. London, Jack, 1876-1916--Homes and haunts--California--Oakland. 2. London, Jack, 1876-1916--Political and social views. 3. Williamson, Eric Miles. 4. Authors, American--20th century--Biography. I. Title.
  PS3523.O46Z9958 2007
  813'.52--dc22
  [B]
                                    2007008813

For my children

Turner Miles Anthony
Guthrie Mitchell
Rosalind Jane
Samantha Marie

Contents

Oakland, Jack London, *and* Me

I

I HATE THE POOR, I LOVE THE POOR, I HATE THEM, I LOVE THEM

A foolish consistency is the hobgoblin of little minds, adored by little statesmen and philosophers and divines. With consistency a great soul has simply nothing to do. He may as well concern himself with his shadow on the wall. Speak what you think now in hard words and to-morrow speak what to-morrow thinks in hard words again, though it contradict every thing you said to-day.—"Ah, so you shall be sure to be misunderstood."—Is it so bad then to be misunderstood? Pythagoras was misunderstood, and Socrates, and Jesus, and Luther, and Copernicus, and Galileo, and Newton, and every pure and wise spirit that ever took flesh. To be great is to be misunderstood.

—Ralph Waldo Emerson

Jack London is misunderstood.

People call him confused. They call him confused because he is both Socialist[1] and Fascist[2]. One day he's preaching on a soapbox in a public square in Oakland, California, about workers' rights and the necessity for revolution, and the next day he's condemning the poor, calling them subhuman beasts who deserve the miserable lives they lead. This is seen as contradiction, a sign that London doesn't know what he thinks of humanity.

This contradiction is seen as a fault, a problem, a sign that London was an inferior thinker.

I'd listen to Emerson on the value of contradiction before I'd listen to literary critics, though. If a thinker has only one opinion, if a writer has only one tale to tell, then there's not much point in reading more than one of his works. A thinker who thinks he has it all figured out is a fool. Every theory mankind has ever believed in, excepting the ones we believe in now, has been disproven. There's no reason to believe that our current theories are correct.

Jack London presents a slight variation on contradiction. He doesn't simply change his mind during the course of his literary career. He believes in clashing theories concurrently. At the same time as believing in helping the poor, in socializing the nation, he believes that they should be crushed like garden slugs underfoot.

Oscar Wilde writes, "The well-bred contradict other people. The wise contradict themselves."

Walt Whitman: "Do I contradict myself? Very well then I contradict myself. (I am large, I contain multitudes)."

William Blake: "The man who never alters his opinion is like standing water, & breeds reptiles of the mind."

Nietzsche: "The thinker needs nobody to refute him: for that he suffices himself," and "How does one compromise oneself today? By being consistent."

And Camus: "Let's suppose a philosopher who after having published several works declares in a new book: 'Up to now I was going in the wrong direction. I am going to begin all over. I think now that I was wrong.' No one would take him seriously any more. And yet he would then be giving proof that he is worthy of thought."

London contradicts himself, and the critics think he's got a problem. One of the sharper London critics, Richard O'Connor, writes:

> Obviously a man in whose thought could be found the elements of latter-day Fascism and Communism, mingled with a peculiarly American dream of success, was suffering from a confusion of the intellect.

This has been the reigning opinion concerning London's thinking for those who have bothered to read more than just his most famous works. Carolyn Johnston, in her 1984 book, *Jack London—An American Radical?*, writes of the way London has been perceived:

> [A]ccounts either resembled tales of corruption by capitalism or portrayed London as a proletarian hero . . . . [I] argue that despite his revolutionary rhetoric and passionate professions of his faith in socialism, his own actions and ideas presented deep contradictions for his radicalism. His socialism can only be adequately understood within the context of his proletarian youth and the important psychological needs which social- ism satisfied for him. He was too individualistic to be involved in daily socialist organizing, and he was too wounded by his own experiences with poverty to ever closely identify with workers as equals. London's ideas, rhetoric and actions were inconsistent. . . .

The reason critics see London's contradictory philosophies as not making sense, as being somehow irreconcilable, is that most of the people who have examined the problem at all really don't know much about working-class poverty.

It's pretty easy to theorize about poverty, to do a field study in a slum, to dissertate about the conditions of the poor en route to a university post. To take a summer job as a col-

lege student doing some kind of manual labor is a nifty break
from the rigors of study for many students.

To think, however, that because you've studied the poverty
of the working poor, to think, for an instant, that just because
you've spent a summer or two digging ditches or canning tuna
or chopping wood or fitting nuts and bolts on an assembly line
you're qualified to speak knowingly about the problems and
conditions of the working poor is kind of like being a slum
dweller and trying to understand the problems of the rich.
For although scholars and voyeurs might be able to *empathize*
and *sympathize* with the poor, although they might be able to
quantify and qualify and identify the problems of the poor,
there ain't no way in hell they're going to be able to *understand*
just what's going on in the hearts of the poor. They're tour-
ists with typewriters. There's just no way to even imagine the
stones of dread that fill the guts of those for whom the cellar
of society is just a falter, a misstep, a mistake, a bad day at
work away. Jack London writes in "What Life Means to Me":

> I had been born in the working-class, and I was now,
> at the age of eighteen, beneath the point at which I
> had started. I was down in the cellar of society, down
> in the subterranean depths of misery about which it is
> neither nice nor proper to speak. I was in the abyss,
> the human cesspool, the shambles and the charnel-
> house of our civilization. This is the part of the edifice
> of society that society chooses to ignore. Lack of space
> compels me here to ignore it, and I shall say only that
> the things I there saw gave me a terrible scare.

A scare is right: he'd seen what every person in the working
class has seen—the consequences of a mistake, what happens
to you if you get fired from your job, if you get sick and can't
work, if you get too old to perform your workhog duties.

When I was just a boy, living in a trailer next to the Texaco gas station for which the man who raised me worked, I got sent home from school one day for getting into a fight. Actually, I was being beaten by a gang of Mexicans who routinely pummeled the dozen or so white boys at the school. The man who raised me, Kent Williamson, took me for a drive. He took me to the very worst areas of Oakland, neighborhoods in which blacks lay on their porches like dogs, wine jugs broken at their feet, houses sagging and unpainted, prostitutes flashing their wares to us as we drove through. Kent stopped the tow truck, made me get out, and he said he'd be back in a minute. He drove off and left me standing there. As his tow truck pulled away, I could feel the eyes of the bums, the whores, the junkies, the angry blacks all following me, eyes that stared through the darkness like creatures from hideous nightmares. I thought I would surely die, and I couldn't move. I just stood there. And when Kent came back—he'd merely driven around the corner—I jumped in the truck and he turned to me and said, "This is where you'll be living if you fuck up in school."

At the lower fringe of the working class the people live with terror in their bones. This terror shimmers all around them, because it's a terror that is entirely justified by their situations. They've seen their friends, their relatives, their siblings and their neighbors descend into "the abyss, the human cesspool."

Jack London's contradictions make complete sense to me. I'm uniquely qualified to write about them. They're my own. In *Jack London—An American Radical?*, Carolyn Johnston says that folks are fascinated with London because he is a mysterious guy:

> Nearly seventy years after Jack London's death, he is
> still shrouded by mystery. No one will ever be able

to prove conclusively the circumstances of either his birth or his death. Perhaps this is one of the reasons he has assumed almost mythic proportions and remains an intriguing and elusive figure.

London isn't interesting because he was born a bastard and died a probable suicide—human degradation isn't the stuff of myth: he's interesting because he represents a curiosity to upper-class folks who can't truly understand poverty and its products, and because he represents hope for lower-class folks who would like to imagine themselves adventuring their way out of their respective hells.

I grew up in Oakland, just blocks from the neighborhood in which Jack London spent his youth. I know the 'hood. Like London, I've chosen the life of the writer as my means out of the ghetto, becoming an academic—a teacher of writing—as literary writing is no longer a means of financial support in America. My family still lives in Oakland. I have a stepbrother who has failed and is in the abyss; the last time anyone heard, he was homeless and dazed on drugs, begging on the streets.

I understand how London feels about the poor, because the problem London tries to work through is the very problem I've been trying to work through my entire life. It's a problem that won't go away.

Professors Cassuto and Reesman, in their Introduction to *Rereading Jack London*, write:

> London struggled mightily as a writer and thinker to understand his world and to change it. As with Emerson—and his representative men—the constant in London's intellectual life was movement. His politics displayed a notorious inconsistency, and the range of his works defies intellectual or generic categorization. Though readers have never had trouble approaching it,

London's work is hard to read critically because of its diversity. Early in his career he successfully opposed the popular magazines' prevailing literary modes of overheated sentimentality with the frigid blast of his radical reconstruction of nature in the Northland. Then came the stories of New Women, racial others, alien cultures, cavemen, and dystopians as chosen centers of consciousness. Throughout, London strives for an ineffable spiritual reality, which he sought most explicitly in his last year, following his reading of C.G. Jung. The primordial vision of the Northland stories is transmuted into his California agrarian dream and then finds its final, but still dynamic, form in the psychological and archetypal Oceanic Paradise Lost with which he ended his career. His only consistency may seem to lie in the volume and power of his barbaric yawp, his effort to know and to be heard, to make himself a force in the world in which he lived.

The essay is one of the better ones around concerning London, its authors attempting to stand back and somewhat objectively look at London's work. However, when they write that London's "politics displayed a notorious inconsistency" and "His only consistency may seem to lie in the volume and power of his barbaric yawp, his effort to know and to be heard, to make himself a force in the world in which he lived," they're missing the boat. They're actively deciding not to understand the most interesting aspect of London—his contradictions. Rather than make an effort at reconciling these contradictions, they dismiss London as a loudmouth standing on the rooftops of the world howling a Whitmanian barbaric yawp.

London's volume, the brassiness of his work, is the scream of a man in terror of his roots. He wants out of the ghetto, but the ghetto won't get *out of him*. Write as he might, no amount of success will ever divorce him completely from The Pit.

Alex Kershaw, in his biography of London, writes:

> Jack was aware that mankind's terror has always been
> its most basic emotion. . . . it has far deeper roots than
> love, tracing back to the days before history, when
> man was just another wild, frightened savage. Fear
> had made Jack escape the ghetto and achieve success.
> It had inspired his most brilliant prose.

The ghetto is always with a writer from the ghetto. It's a
looming presence and the primary, if not the only, motivator
for such writers.

My own route out of the ghetto, I decided after being fired
from a construction job (the foreman's son pulled a knife on
me and I had a shovel in my hand—I clobbered him upside the
head—his hardhat probably kept me from going to jail) and
finding myself unemployed and living out of my car, was to
go to college and become a college teacher. I was going to live
my life in the Ivory Tower, where no black and Mexican gangs
would supply me with a daily beating, where only the driven, the
intelligent, and the superior portion of humanity would be my
comrades. Imagine my surprise when I achieved my goal, when
I landed my first full-time teaching job at an urban community
college. I had eight years of college under my belt, a bachelor's
degree, a masters degree, my coursework for a second masters
complete. I was ready to live in the Ivory Tower, to have done
with the ghetto forever. Imagine my surprise when I walked into
the classroom and surveyed the students I was to teach. They
were wearing headphones; they were cursing and throwing
things at each other; they were stoned, coked-up, pregnant with
welfare babies, eating Big Macs, staring dully ahead as if being in
the classroom was a torture and a burden. Junkies sat in the back
of the room scratching themselves like dogs with fleas. Guns
fell out of purses, and I pretended not to notice. I was the only

Caucasian in the room. I assigned a diagnostic essay, and five of the students walked out of the class, one saying, "Fuck you, whitey," as he departed.

Over the years, it got worse. Two of our teachers were shot. I had a knife pulled on me by a student because I asked him why he had spat on my truck. "I cut you up, motherfuck white ass honkey son bitch. I cut you up," he explained. After class each Friday I signed welfare forms and parole forms so that the young scholars could prove to their supervisors that they'd been attending class. These students were from my neighborhood, from families like or better than mine, but they were not like me. Their educations were federally funded, there being programs which pay colleges to take in the dregs of society, the criminals and junkies and welfare cases. By the end of my stay there, when I walked into the classroom I felt nauseous, my throat filled with bile.

I'd spent seven years on construction sites and eight years in college trying to escape The Abyss, and I found myself right back in it, teaching the very beasts from whom I'd been trying to separate myself. My last year at the college, I carried an eighteen-inch machete in my book bag, just in case. I was so frantic with the need to get away from the beasts, from the bottom feeders of humanity, that I quit my coveted position, sold my vehicles, cashed out my retirement, sold all my possessions except my books and computer, and moved to New York to try again to escape, to move up the ladder by attending a private university. I would have done anything. My soul was for sale. By the end of my third year in New York City I was broke and living in Queens, where my neighbors carved swastikas into the hood of my car.

The poor? I hate them with all my soul. Welfare recipients should be sent to Nevada, fenced in, and forced to build pyramids for their room and board.

The poor? I love them with everything that's me. I cheer when riots topple cities, when the poor ravage the homes of the rich.

I hate them because they don't have the drive I do. I love them because I'm one of them.

O'Connor writes, "The motive force that drove him to produce fifty books in the sixteen years of his professional career was an unquenchable desire for success and all its rewards." O'Connor just doesn't get it. London isn't striving for success. He's running from failure. And there's a hell of a big difference.

No amount of success can eliminate the fear of failure from the mind of someone who started out in the ghetto.

When I began writing this book, I was writing for my life. If I didn't finish it, I lost my job at San Jose State University. If I lost my job at San Jose State, it was back to digging ditches for me.

I joined the Laborers Local Union #304, Oakland, California, when I turned eighteen. I worked the nastiest jobs imaginable for seven years. When I got my first full-time teaching job, laboring at the community college in Houston, Texas, I lay down my hammer and trowel and hardhat. But I never let my union card expire.

I pay my seventeen dollars a month religiously. I never miss my dues. Because I know that at any moment in my life I could be thrust back down to the laboring classes.

But I'm getting old now. And I might not be able to perform the duties of the laborer.

Logically, I knew that if I didn't finish this book I wouldn't end up homeless. I would find something to do to earn me a living.

But in my bones, in my soul, I feared The Abyss, and still do. I see myself staggering the streets of the cities, drunk out of my mind on Thunderbird or Night Train, sleeping in doorways and digging through garbage cans for food. I see bums on the street and fear that if I screw up even slightly, I'll end up their colleague. I see myself on the street where Kent dropped me off when I was a little boy in Oakland.

Jack London has this same fear. When he wakes up each morning to write his famous thousand words per day, he fears that if he doesn't get that thousand, he's on his way down to The Abyss. And he writes that thousand words no matter what: when he was cruising his yacht, *The Snark*, he caught a tropical disease and swelled up like a bloated corpse, his skin peeling off in layers, his hands puffed up like catcher's mitts. Sick with disease, he writes *Success* (later to become *Martin Eden*), the novel *Adventure*, and several of the stories later collected in *When God Laughs*, *The Night Born*, and *The Human Drift*. After the publication of *The People of the Abyss*, London's book about the squalor of London, England's East End ghetto, a reviewer for *Bookman* in 1904 complains that London "needs must assure the reader that in his own home he is accustomed to carefully prepared food and good clothes and daily tub—a fact that he might safely have left to be taken for granted." But these *facts* are not facts for London, no matter how rich he gets. As his daughter, Joan London, writes:

> Jack London had escaped too recently from the squalor and insecurity of the working class to be able to take such a fact for granted, and, by the same token, had far less need to assure his readers of his comfortable status than himself. Scenes of his youth, distorted by the ugliness he was seeing on every side, had returned to torment him, and only by reiterating the difference between his present good fortune and that of the dwellers in the Abyss could he lull his panic at the thought that one day he might be poor and a casual laborer again.

He's driven by terror. He makes his million, buys ever more acres, tries to create a self-sustaining ranch, labors to free himself from the powers of man and nature. He's terrified that at any instant he will lose it all, will be stripped of the fruits of his labors and cast down into hell. In "How I Became a Socialist," London writes of this work ethic:

> Work was everything. It was sanctification and salvation. The pride I took in a hard day's work well done would be inconceivable to you. It is almost inconceivable to me as I look back upon it. I was as faithful a wage slave as ever capitalist exploited. To shirk or malinger on the man who paid me my wages was a sin, first, against myself, and second, against him. I considered it a crime second only to treason and just about as bad.

This is his early attitude, the strong and pure blue-collar work ethic.

But he finds, as do all blue-collar workers, that his work actually works against him, for he is making the capitalists increasingly rich, empowering them more, enabling them to become so powerful that it is much easier for them to exploit the workers beneath them either directly or indirectly. At the same time as being a working machine, London is well aware of the benefactors of his labors. In his essay "What Life Means to Me," he writes:

> I never got the full product of my toil. I looked at the daughter of the cannery owner, in her carriage, and knew that it was my muscle, in part, that helped drag along that carriage on its rubber tires. I looked at the son of the factory owner, going to college, and knew that it was my muscle that helped, in part, to pay for the wine and good fellowship he enjoyed.

You'll never find more fanatical workers than among those who have escaped what we condescendingly call the "working class": if they've escaped, they don't quite trust the fact, and they work at their typewriters and desks as if they're shoveling coal into the furnace of a hungry locomotive. Although he liberates himself from working for others, London's attitude toward work remains the same throughout his life. He becomes what he calls a "brain merchant," selling his thoughts, but he still believes, like a good blue-collar citizen, that work is the end-all. In his essay "Getting into Print," he writes, "And work. Spell it in capital letters, WORK. Work all the time."

Jack London signs his letters, "Yours for the revolution."

He also says, "The reason a man works for me is because he cannot work for himself. Stupid boobs, most of them!"

To most people these two attitudes are in conflict.

They make perfect sense to me.

By the end of this book, they should make sense to you, too.

Notes

[1] In London's essay "The Question of the Maximum," we find his take on Marxist Socialist theory of social development. It is a virtual re-rendering of what we find in *The Communist Manifesto* and *Das Kapital*. From the beginning of the essay:

> For any social movement or development there must be a maximum limit beyond which it cannot proceed. That civilization which does not advance must decline, and so, when the maximum of development has been reached in any given direction, society must either retrograde or change the direction of its advance. There are many families of men that have failed, in the critical period of their economic evolution, to effect a change in direction, and were forced to fall back. Vanquished at the moment of their maximum, they have dropped out of the whirl of the world. There was no room for them. Stronger competitors have taken their places, and they have either rotted into oblivion or remain to be crushed under the iron heel of the dominant races in as remorseless a struggle as the world has yet witnessed. But in this struggle fair women and chivalrous men will play no part. Types and ideals have changed. Helens and Launcelots are anachronisms. Blows will be given and taken, and men fight and die, but not for faiths and altars. Shrines will be desecrated, but they will be the shrines, not of temples, but market-places. Prophets will arise, but they will be the prophets of prices and products. Battles will be waged, not for honor and glory, nor for thrones and sceptres, but for dollars and cents and for marts and exchanges. Brain and not brawn will endure, and the captains of war will be commanded by the captains of industry. In short, it will be a contest for the mastery of the world's commerce and for industrial supremacy.

And from the conclusion:

> When capitalistic production has attained its maximum development, it must confront a dividing of the ways; and the strength of capital on the one hand, and the education and wisdom of the workers on the other, will determine which path society is to travel. It is possible, considering the inertia of the masses, that the whole world might in time come to be dominated by a group of industrial oligarchies, or by one great oligarchy, but it is not probable. That sporadic oligarchies may flourish for definite periods of time is highly possible; that they may continue to do so is as highly improbable. The procession of the ages has marked not only the rise of man, but the rise of the common man. From the chattel slave, or the serf chained to the soil, to the highest seats in modern society, he has risen, rung by rung, amid the crumbling of the divine right of kings and the crash of falling sceptres. That he has done this, only in the end to pass into the perpetual slavery of the industrial oligarch, is something at which his whole past cries in protest. The common man is worthy of a better future, or else he is not worthy of his past.

[2] O'Connor cites London as saying, "A superman's chiefest danger is his fellow supermen. The great stupid mass of people did not count." As well, O'Connor cites Lewis Mumford's 1926 book, *The Golden Day*, in which Mumford blasted London, his novel *The Sea Wolf*, and its main character, Wolf Larsen:

> Mumford charged that London even "clung to socialism, it would seem, chiefly to give an additional luster of braggadocio and romanticism to his career; for socialism, to London's middle-class contemporaries, was

an adventure more desperate than the rush for gold in the Klondike . . . he betrayed his socialism in all his ingrained beliefs, particularly his belief in success, and in his conception of the Superman."

. . . "The career of the Superman in America is an instructive spectacle," Mumford wrote. "He sprang, this overman, out of the pages of Emerson; it was Emerson's way of expressing the inexhaustible evolutionary possibilities of a whole race of Platos, Michalangelos, and Montaignes. Caught up by Nietzsche, and colored by the dark natural theology Darwin had inherited from Malthus, the Superman became the highest possibility of natural selection; he served as a symbol of contrast with the cooperative or 'slave morality' of Christianity. The point to notice is that in both Emerson and Nietzsche the Superman is a higher type: the mark of his genius is the completer development of his human capacities . . . London, however, seized the suggestion of the Superman and attempted to turn it into reality. And what did he become? Nothing less than a preposterous bully . . . like his whole gallery of brutal and brawny men—creatures blessed with nothing more than the gift of a magnificent animality, and the absence of a social code which would prevent them from inflicting this gift upon their neighbors. In short, London's Superman was little more than the infantile dream of the messenger boy or the barroom tough or the nice, respectable clerk whose muscles will never quite stand up under the strain. He was the social platitude of the old West, translated into a literary epigram."

II

THE ACADEMIC TREATMENT OF LONDON

1

In 1898 Jack London sold his first short story to a San Francisco-based magazine, *Overland Monthly*, for five dollars. A year later, he landed "Odyssey of the North" with *Atlantic Monthly*, and from there he went on to become the first American author to become a millionaire through his writing, to become America's most famous author—a celebrity akin to a movie star of today. London remains the best-selling American author in the world. According to James Lundquist in his book *Jack London: Adventures, Ideas, and Fiction*:

> The demand for London's books did not stop with his death, and at least twelve volumes (one as late as 1972) were published posthumously in English. His popularity, particularly abroad, has diminished little, and London remains the best-selling American writer world-wide. Nearly eight million copies of *The Call of the Wild* have been sold since 1903 [Lundquist is writing this in 1987], his work has been translated into over sixty languages, and in the Soviet Union there are nine separate editions of his collected work.

Robert Barltrop, in his book *Jack London: the Man, the Writer, the Rebel,* also believes that London should not be dismissed, noting that London's books are still, now over ninety years since his death, "reprinted throughout the literate world." He writes, "If a writer continues to give satisfaction to large numbers of people for a long enough period, he becomes entitled to a place of respect in literature."

London's general treatment by the academic community, however, has been less than respectful. The English professorate in America has only recently deigned to acknowledge his works as something worthy of study in any fashion other than biographically. Earle Labor, the scholar who has done the most legwork on London (compiling London's short stories, compiling London's letters, editing numerous collections including Viking's *The Portable Jack London*), writes in his essay "Jack London's *Mondo Cane*":

> One explanation for this kind of critical neglect, generally speaking, lies in the very skill with which London made all his stories—dog and otherwise—so easy to read. . . . We tend to disparage that which is effortless, and the tendency to assume that by and large the value of reading matter is proportionate to the amount of difficulty it offers manifests itself frequently in literary criticism and scholarship. The perennial critical appeal of such fictionists as Henry James and William Faulkner, for example, is undoubtedly due in some measure to the intricacies of their styles as well as to the intrinsic literary merit which their works possess. In other words, their works offer an intellectual challenge to the critical puzzle-solver which is not necessarily related to literary value judgments. Moreover, by giving the critic a vital role as interpretive mediator, they keep him in business.

Labor's assessment of the critical situation with regard to London's work, as well as his views of critical endeavor at large, seems reasonable enough. Proust's *A la recherche du temps perdu*, a book I've tried to read three times and never made it past page 1500, generates glee among a bevy of academics, though even Richard Howard—in his heart a poet—who has translated nearly 200 volumes of literature from the French, couldn't muster up the energy to translate past the first of the book's seven volumes. Gertrude Stein, James Joyce, and T. S. Eliot generate ten articles per every article on John Steinbeck, Robert Frost, and Willa Cather, and the reason is pretty simple: the former triumvirate is linguistically more difficult than the latter trio. Though simply written, George's dilemma at the end of *Of Mice and Men* is far more poignant than Eliot's chant, "This is the way the world ends." The simplicity of Sinclair Lewis, of Cather, of London, doesn't provide contemporary academic critics, who increasingly see themselves in the position of Translators to English from the English, with much to do.

Thomas Pynchon's tome, *Gravity's Rainbow*, has become an industry, and though the linguistic fireworks of the book are impressive indeed, who can read the thing? Gaddis's *JR* is brilliant, certainly, but in the final analysis it just might be more work to read than is worth the while. In academia, however, these books dwarf the Nobel Prize efforts of Sinclair Lewis, of Steinbeck, of Pearl S. Buck, and the efforts of Jack London. They need *translation*.

Until recently, London has been viewed as a curiosity, as a writer of popular fiction in the adventure genre who happened a couple of times to mysteriously knock out a good story, a story which nearly, but not quite, measured up to American academic aesthetic standards. The "good" stories are the ones which create the need for translation, for solving the unsolvable moral dilemmas presented. "Odyssey of the North," "To Build a Fire," *The Call of the Wild*, and *White Fang* have generated periodic condescending or crude careerist interest—professors writing about his work because it was an "open field" and generated an easy publication—but London's work—again, until recently—has been for the most part shunned. As a college student, I took over sixty courses, undergraduate and graduate, in literature, and only once was I required to read Jack London. Compare this with the twelve times I had to read *The Scarlet Letter*, the eight times I had to read Frederick Douglass's slave narrative, the eight times I read *The Great Gatsby*. Henry James' *The American*—five times. The six times I was force-fed Richard Wright's *Black Boy*. I had to suffer through Harriet Beecher Stowe's *Uncle Tom's Cabin* four times. During the fourteen years of my college education, Jack London wasn't, to my recollection, even mentioned in a classroom until the late James Tuttleton at New York University assigned *The Call of the Wild* to a class in American realism and naturalism.

There are readily identifiable reasons why London has been kept off the reading lists and syllabi. London's Socialism has not been in vogue, and professors reared in the fifties and tenured in the sixties have shunned London like they have Dos Passos, Steinbeck, and Sinclair Lewis. London was an outspoken racist, and, of course, this will not do: evolutionist theories are applied to everything except modern mankind, as we live in touchy times as far as that goes. His essay "The Yellow Peril," a xenophobic rant against the Japanese and the threat they posed to the West, is often cited as evidence of his racism—never mind the fact that he was *right* to fear the Japanese, who, a generation later, invaded China, bombed Pearl Harbor, enslaved the Koreans, and proved to be some of the most vicious defilers of humanity recent history has witnessed. London aggressively distances himself from the Eastern literary establishment, which, undoubtedly, would never have taken in a ghetto boy from Oakland anyway. The Eastern literary establishment, led during London's time by William Dean Howells, Henry James and the like, was (as it still is) a club based largely on New York, Boston, and the Ivies. This club allowed a writer like Stephen Crane, whose prose is some of the worst in American literary history, to become a darling; and indeed, Crane's deplorably sophomoric and ridiculously written "The Open Boat" is still standard fare for undergraduate and graduate students of literature alike. Crane, of course, was sponsored by James and Howells. Also working against London in recent times is his machismo: he is a *man*—a man who hunted and fished and labored and felt there was a difference between men and women. This has not served him well. Witness the treatment Hemingway has received in recent years: scores of articles have been written about what a disgusting macho cad Hemingway was, many of the critics accusing Hemingway of being a latent homosexual. Being a man, in the traditional sense of the word, has worked against London, and, like Hemingway, he has begun to undergo the Genderists and Queer Theorists's finger wagging: "Jack's a latent homosexual!" The list goes on: he is white, male, racist, macho, sexist, anti-intellectual, fascist, communist, mercenary, aesthetically simplistic, poorly educated, a drunkard, a showboat, a hypocrite. Those who would promote a literary canon based on aesthetic principles scoff at London's supposedly stone-mitted style and crude autodidacticism, and those who would base entry into the canon on political considerations deplore London for his failure to espouse the tenets of today's supra-democratic aesthetic liberalism. No matter what your cause, you won't have to look hard to find something to hate about Jack London. London is everything contemporary academics despise. Which is why, in the past decade, he has come back into vogue—not as a literary figure, but as a literary whipping boy.

No easier target has ever taken up the pen in this country, and in the climate of hatred (hatred for the canon, hatred for white males, hatred for those who aren't white males, hatred for those who would reconfigure the canon, hatred for aesthetics and for anti-aesthetics, and so forth) which characterizes the universally fractured English departments around the country, London is a writer who can be trotted out, shoved to his knees, and flogged without letup and without objection. For those who would seek an icon of the White Male Oppressor, they need look no further than London: he's a crowd pleaser for Marxists, Feminists, Multiculturalists, African-Americanists, Postcolonialists, and the practitioners of the rest of the isms which pluralize literary sump tanks today.

Jack London is a didactic writer—his works drip and ooze with the theses he presents—but the lessons he teaches are scorned today. White males of the past are allowed didacticism only if it falls within certain parameters—it must deal with aesthetics, or it must deal with the oppressions of women, of darker-skinned peoples, of politically oppressed peoples. Hence we read Voltaire, but not Steinbeck; Ralph Ellison, but not Dos Passos; Kate Chopin, but not Sinclair Lewis; Langston Hughes, but not Ezra Pound (Steinbeck, Dos Passos, Lewis, and Pound all being writers whose work I was never assigned in college). Henry Miller—one of the most important influences on 20th-century American writers—well, Miller is American literature's dirty little secret. An awesome force in terms of his sway over the spawn of writers who follow in his wake, Miller, who just may be the greatest American author of the 20th century, is considered a dirty, nasty man, a racist and sexist who is beneath mention—in academia, at least. The Nigerian writer Chinua Achebe attacks Joseph Conrad's *Heart of Darkness* and concludes that "Conrad was a thoroughgoing racist," making no distinction between Conrad and the narrator of the novel, claiming implicitly that no work can be a masterpiece if, when its politics are scrutinized, it is found to be offensive, and the academy nods in sober and timid agreement, for Achebe has spoken what is expected of him. He has spoken the fashionable party line. Masterpieces are scrutinized for hints of racism, sexism, elitism, and so forth, and when the offense is detected, the author is denounced. When the works don't supply the necessary information for the dismantling of an author's reputation, the critics turn to biography. As Jonathan Auerbach writes,

> Set in the primitive wilderness of the frozen North, city ghettos, or exotic seas; self-consciously infused with the evolutionist rhetoric of Herbert Spenser; and drawing on the adventuring author's elemental manhood, Jack London's writings have become perfect grist for a certain kind of critical mill—a romantic model that runs all the more smoothly by treating his life experience as a kind of validating second nature spontaneously called up during the writing process.

London's biography serves as a launching point for harangues *against* London, *against* anything that London can be linked to, remotely or otherwise. He wrote what he thought, and sometimes what he thought was unpleasant.

He's paying the price.

2

Although recently, as scholars scramble like corporate executives for new critical niches ("untapped markets" to exploit for publication, consequent promotions, pay raises, sabbaticals, et cetera), there has been a renewed "interest" in Jack London's work (as there has been in scads of other "neglected" authors), most of this interest has focused on a handful of short stories ("Odyssey of the North," "To Build a Fire," and "The White Silence" are the most popular) and the most important of London's novels, namely *Martin Eden*, *The Sea Wolf*, *The Call of the Wild*, *The People of the Abyss*, *The Road*, and *The Iron Heel*.

But by and large London's work has been as ignored critically as it has been in the anthologies, critics preferring to apply current critical stances such as Marxist Theory, Feminist Theory, and Postcolonial Theory to the most obviously applicable of London's works. Earle Labor, one of the first scholarly critics to devote his life's work to the study of London, provides a thorough and up-to-date review of London criticism in his "Afterword: The Representative Man as Writer/Hero," appended to Leonard Cassuto's *Rereading Jack London*. As well, Mr. Labor provides a review of criticism in Chapter Six, "A Man for Many Literary Seasons," which closes his 1994 revised edition of the seminal *Jack London*. Labor's *Jack London* remains the most useful introduction to serious study of London and his work, masterfully blending critical reading and biographical research into a book which without agenda is both comprehensive and dignified.

Jonathan Auerbach, in his recent book, *Male Call: Becoming Jack London,* sums up current Jack London criticism thusly:

Currently there are two to three times as many biographies of London as book-length critical examinations of his work; I cannot think of another American author, canonical or otherwise, for whom this holds true. The pull toward biography in London studies has been so strong, in fact, that it is difficult to conceive of a way of critically interpreting his work that does not assume the concept of a personal career as the organizing principle of analysis. Whether the emphasis falls on his socialism, his Klondike tales, or later fiction set in Hawaii, reading his writing at times quickly gives way to chronological descriptions of his life, with plot summary all too often substituting for textual analysis, as if meaning were self-evident, simply the factual documentation of London's personal experience.

He's right, and as Jack London, until recently, has not been universally recognized as an American "literary" figure (note that Harold Bloom does not mention London even once in his book *The Western Canon*), there is not much scholarly work which deals with the author before the great university expansion era of the 1960s. Early work on London consists primarily of a healthy selection of biographies, notably those of London's wife, Charmian; his daughter, Joan; his fellow socialite, Georgia Loring Bamford; and the first thorough biography, that of Richard O'Connor. Consequent of London's being shunned by the past generation's major critics, the early Jack London criticism suffers from the relatively simplistic approaches of minor critics and academics, the likes of which we find in Ray Wilson Ownbey's "Introduction: London in the Seventies," which introduces his 1978 collection of critical essays. These early critical looks at London generally fall into two categories: biographical summary and heartfelt defense. The biographical summaries of London's work generally

examine a work of London's and then show the correspondences or lack of correspondences with what is known of
London's actual life. Critical analysis is all but absent in these
articles, useful as they may be for the student of biographic
correspondences. The second type of early critical approaches
dealing with London is that of the defense, the argument that
London be included among those American writers studied
at the university level. These sometimes passionate arguments try to make the case that London, though neglected in
the academic community, is a writer worthy of study. These
studies generally operate thusly: they first establish a set of
aesthetic criteria with which to judge a work of art; then they
apply, usually rather loosely, those criteria to London's works;
the articles generally conclude with a rather summary judgment in London's favor. Ownbey's "Introduction" is a case
in point:

> A short story should have a good narrative. It should
> read well. It should be written in lucid and graphic
> style. It should deal with singular incidents and only a
> few characters. Too many people, too many places and
> too many things take it out of the realm of the short
> story into the realm of longer fiction. Most short stories
> should contain a strong element of irony. As a matter
> of fact, most of the great short stories of the world do
> have a strong ironic twist. Stories like de Maupassant's
> "The Necklace" or "A Piece of String" or Hardy's
> "The Three Strangers" live almost entirely upon
> ironical situations. And yet in none of these stories is
> there stronger irony than in some of London's stories.
>   A short story, when it includes description, must
> have strong and vivid description. London had the
> ability to create a strong narrative, to create marvelous
> story atmosphere, to infuse into it graphic descriptions

that pertain to the characters or the events. But most
of all, he could develop an ironical situation that, upon
analysis, touches each of our lives.

As should be rather obvious, the criteria Ownbey lays out
here are ill-defined. He says that a short story should have "a
good narrative" and that it should "read well," but he does not
define just what constitutes a "good narrative," nor does he
define what he means by a story "reading well"; he doesn't define "lucid" or "graphic"; and even had he *defined* the terms,
he makes no attempt to justify just why these qualities are
necessary for success in a short story. He then takes his cue
from Poe and says that the short story "should deal with sin-
gular incidents," not defining this or justifying its necessity;
and then he uses ideas from Greek drama to claim that a short
story should have "only a few characters," since "Too many
people, too many places and too many things take it out of the
realm of the short story and into the realm of longer fiction."
However, even these criteria are left loose and baggy. Striking especially is Ownbey's claim, "Most short stories should
contain a strong element of irony," and that "most of the great
short stories of the world . . . have a strong ironic twist." The
trick ending, he seems to be saying, is the criteria for short
story greatness—making O. Henry perhaps the greatest modern writer, it would seem, eclipsing Hemingway, Faulkner,
Joyce, and Flannery O'Connor. De Maupassant leaps forward
ahead of Flaubert, and Chopin dwarfs Melville. Ownbey's attempt to launch London to the forefront of letters, given the
criteria he uses, if anything, backfires.

Since Ownbey's time—a full academic generation ago—
criticism has greatly changed. The factionalism of today's
literary climate and criticism is well represented in Leonard
Cassuto's *Rereading Jack London*, a collection of pertinent

contemporary essays. Cassuto's selection of current London criticism is typical of the field of study—a doggie bag of trendy theories applied to London's work. The criticism skims over London's work in favor of theorizing, and much of the stuff reads like it could be applied to a plethora of author's works with precisely the same conclusions. In other words, much of the criticism being written on London's work is canned, prefabricated, assembly-line critique. Scott Derrick's "Making a Heterosexual Man: Gender, Sexuality, and Narrative in the Fiction of Jack London" asserts as its main point,

> London employs a narrative teleology aimed at the construction of heterosexual masculinity to repress and marginalize a finally unacceptable and disruptive homoeroticism. As a consequence, the homoerotic in London's fiction suggests the difficulty of articulating the otherness of the body and its desires, and hence the problem of the unconscious.

Derrick goes on to give the usual schtick, claiming that London was probably a homosexual hiding his queerness from the world underneath the guise of macho. The first subheading of the article—"Cross-Dressing, Cross-Behaving, and Gender Difference"—lets us know all we need to know about the article.

Sam S. Baskett in his article "Sea Change in 'The Sea Wolf'" makes the same claim: London was a homosexual. The essay latches onto a couple of passing phrases and argues that London was an androgynous, latent homosexual. The key phrase, cited from London's letters, is this: "the woman in me pleads, but my manhood reasons." Therefore (after much predictable jargon) London is gay.

Other recent critics follow the Derridian/Foucaultesque/Semiotic bent, and reduce London's work to codes and signs and signifiers and crank out five or ten thousand words on the dissection of a phrase—all of which critical calisthenics is rather funny, actually, considering that London was one of America's least careful prose writers, letting editors change what they would, never revising, hammering out a thousand words a day before breakfast every day of his working life. Check out Francis Schor in "Power, Gender, and Ideological Discourse in *The Iron Heel*":

> The interconnection here of ideological discourse, images, and language is illuminated by French sociolinguist Michel Pecheux's contention: "The meaning of a word, an expression, a proposition, etc. doesn't exist 'in itself,' but is determined by the ideological positions brought into play in the socio-historical process in which words, expressions, and propositions are produced." Thus, by identifying how London's ideological discourse emerges out of the context, one can better discern the sociohistorical meanings of power and gender in *The Iron Heel*.

The article then goes on for several pages about "Jackson's arm," reducing the sweep of London's vast vision to a couple of words, attempting to shrink London's scope down to the type of synecdoche practiced by poets. This kind of microscrutiny of London's work is, quite frankly, preposterous, since analyzing London word by word is akin to performing an etymological analysis of the language of a translation. Even if London did actually use the specific words under scrutiny, their use was, more likely than not, not well considered. London was concerned with *stories*.

There are some other real stretchers out there. James Williams, in his article "Commitment and Practice: The Authorship of Jack London," does a postmodern dance, attempting to prove that London was not merely self-referential in that he wrote of his own experience and thinly veiled the semi-autobiographical heroes of his novels, but that London was also a self-referential writer along the lines of the postmodernists (and Sterne long ago!) such as John Barth, Ronald Sukenick, Peter Handke, and so forth. Williams writes, "Because the figure of the liar or tall-tale teller is so often linked in London's work to the artist, we can take this story ["Nam-Bok the Unveracious"] as a fable of manuscript rejection." The stretch from a story about storytelling and myth-making on the Yukon Delta, about survival and about the contrast between European culture and Eskimo culture, about the difference between primitive culture and industrialized culture, to a story about getting one's short stories rejected by publishers, is a long stretch indeed. I've read the story a good many times now, and, as the boy said about the Emperor's New Clothes, I just don't see it.

Along the same lines, Jonathan Auerbach, in his essay "Congested Mails: Buck and Jack's 'Call,'" also reduces London, as per a postmodern critical fad, to a self-referential postmodernist:

> Buck has been associated with writing, from the very first sentence of the story [The Call of the Wild]. . . . This is certainly a strange way to introduce a dog-hero, making Buck's (not) reading seem a matter of preference, rather than possibility. . . . The result is a trace of Buck's understanding print, as if the news of the Klondike gold strike that occasions his subsequent captivity is somehow available to him, as if he verges on knowing what he cannot know. Literalizing in this way the operations of the unconscious, London positions Buck midway between a passive sign to be read and a reader of signs himself.
>
> The most important link between Buck and writing concerns his work itself, his toiling in the traces to deliver letters.

So Jack London wasn't really writing a Nietzschean/Darwinian allegorical story about a dog and the Northland; no, behind what we might foolishly perceive to be the story of *The Call of the Wild*, London was cleverly hiding his true intent: to write about writing.

And Auerbach does not fail to take his potshots at London:

> If this novel [*The Call of the Wild*] is an allegory at all, in fact, it should be read as an uncanny anticipation of the course of London's professional "calling," his great popularity—starting with the publication of *The Call of the Wild*—as well as his subsequent struggles to maintain and manage his success in the literary marketplace. Striking it rich, London takes revenge on his public—he does not stop writing, as Buck stops working; instead, the disenchanted London is driven, drives himself, to write more, to write about himself, about his own fame, over and over again until he eventually breaks down.

London, instead of writing because he is a writer, instead of writing because it has been his passion since he was a teenager, instead of writing because he has things to say and he wants to make the world a better place through the dissemination of philosophies he considers to be sound and useful for the betterment of mankind, now, according to Auerbach, writes *for revenge*, because he wants to *torture* the American population with his drivel. Note how London's "breakdown" is attributed to his *writing too much*, and not to his drinking, his raw meat eating, his bouts with disease in the South Pacific, his laboring youth and the terrible working conditions of 19th-century industrialized America. This is the kind of snide attack that seems to make so many critics giddy.

Clarice Stasz's essay "Social Darwinism, Gender, and Humor in 'Adventure'" slams London for his insensitive, colonialist politics. Predictably, the article reads like Achebe's thrashing of Conrad's *Heart of Darkness*:

> Jack London reached adulthood during the tumult of American imperialism. In 1893, historian Frederick Turner stunned the public with his thesis that the American frontier was closed; quite naturally some responded by urging American incursions abroad. Within the next few years the country would gain Hawaii (through a bloodless coup led by conservative businessmen) and become a major influence in the Philippines and Panama. Although both economic and Christian missionary interests spurred these advances, the ideology of Social Darwinism provided the rationale.
>
> As popularized at the time, Social Darwinism was reduced to a crude argument claiming the survival of the fittest among individuals within a society, and among societies as well. The doctrine appealed to the privileged Anglo-Saxon elite because it reinforced ethnocentric and evolutionist attitudes toward so-called primitive peoples.

Stasz (who wrote the biography of Charmian and Jack London, *American Dreamers*, in which she attributes Jack's success to Charmian) argues that London stinks as both a writer and a human being, and her simplistic arguments (such as Darwin being the driving force behind imperialism—as if conquering other peoples is a recent and specifically American thing) derive whatever force they might accrue from a gallery of yea-saying critics nodding like metronomes to her mantra, "London is a racist." Part of London's works' "failure as literature," she claims, is his "outmoded ideology"—another critic assuming that literature is defined by the academic ideology of the day.

Only contemporary critics, cramming their political agendas into works of art for self-serving purposes, wrenching around a text for the purpose of making it fit a preconceived programme, would be able to perform the kind of alchemical transformation we find in Robert Peluso's "Gazing at Royalty: Jack London's 'The People of the Abyss' and the Emergence of American Imperialism," a postcolonial look at London's muckraking Socialist examination of the people of London's East End slums. The twist: London, an American Colonialist/Imperialist looking at a falling colonial power, England. In this essay, Peluso maintains that it was London's trip to the East End slums that changed London into a radical Socialist. Peluso writes:

> Chronologically, his experiences in the East End took place between his early socialist phase of the 1890s, which was typified by a reformist and parliamentarian view, and the more confrontational version of 1905–11 in which, at least in theory, London's stance was more revolutionary. Viewed against this turn toward an outspoken radicalism, the experiences recorded in *The People of the Abyss* seem to announce the pivotal middle moment in Jack London's political philosophy. The "conversion" to socialism that London spells out in "How I Became a Socialist," although apparently the result of events prior to his trip to the East End, was more likely caused by the head-on confrontation, which he had already described in *People*, with the urban underclass there.

Peluso implies here, of course, with his quotation marks around the word "conversion," that London wasn't a Socialist after all, that he was a poseur, an opportunist. This ad hominem attack continues throughout the article, Peluso rather naively focusing on "How I Became a Socialist" as the end-all answer to the causes behind London's ideologies. By focus-

ing exclusively on *The People of the Abyss*, Peluso facilitates
his thesis, which is that London, although claiming to be a
Socialist, is instead just another imperialist pig. Peluso seems
to forget that London was called "The Boy Socialist" in the
Bay Area papers when he was not more than a teenager. He
neglects what even the most cursory study of Socialism would
reveal: that Socialism is the battle standard for the poor in
any industrialized, stratified society, and that London, a product himself of the ghetto, even if looking upon the ghetto
with revulsion, is constantly aware that it is the miasma of
the ghetto which spawned him. For the purposes of cranking
out a trendy, politically acceptable and correct-thinking paper,
Peluso manipulates London's well-documented philosophical
and sociological stances to serve his own polemic ends. He
goes on, hoping to drive his point home that London is a
condescending imperialist, to attack the language London
uses to describe the ghetto-dwellers:

> The East End inhabitants are designated a "race"
> or "breed" apart by virtue of their difference from
> sturdy Americans. Beginning as a comment on "class
> supremacy." . . . The East End, he says, teems with
> "a deteriorated stock" continually weakened as "the
> strong men, the men of pluck, initiative, and ambition,
> have been faring forth to the fresher and freer por-
> tions of the globe, to make new lands and nations."

Never mind that London often describes himself, in his
laboring days, as a "work beast." Never mind that London
knows all too well that he is merely a work beast made good,
a work beast who has escaped the place he describes in "What
Life Means to Me" as "the cellar of society, . . . the subterranean depths of misery . . . the abyss, the human cesspool,
the shambles and the charnel-house of our civilization." If

London grew up in a "cesspool," then what is he? Human shit. London doesn't place himself above people he describes in animal terms if he sees himself as a turd. Like a host of other contemporary critics, Peluso latches onto a phrase or two that has the capacity to offend our refined and enlightened sensibilities and then works away at attacking not the work of art itself, but the author of the work of art. And he does so without presenting a critical counterpoint, without bothering to suggest that perhaps, just maybe, the conditions of ghettos do indeed cause humanity to suffer monstrous deformities, to undergo actual physical changes due to lack of proper nutrition, lack of medical attention, lack of even the most basic of human necessities.

When people for generation after generation are born and raised and become parents living in a virtual toxic waste dump, they don't represent the finest specimens of humanity after a while. Take a walk in Manhattan's Hell's Kitchen sometime: there, amid famous poverty, you find more dwarves per square mile than I've ever seen in my life. Blind people, cripples, deaf-mutes, a man who stands on the corner of 9th Avenue and 46th Street with no nose—only two holes in the front of his face—and a cyst the size of a softball ready to explode puffed from the side of his neck, the pizza delivery boy with three fingerlike dowels of flesh wagging from an arm cut off at the elbow, people that look like survivors of a nuclear war. Then take a walk through Battery Park City: where are the dwarves? Where the people with stunted limbs? Where are the human monsters? It's fine and dandy to criticize a writer for elitism, but when the facts, and not the politically correct hopes, are examined, there's something to the observation that poverty breeds deformity and debasement.

Only an academic critic could turn one of the strongest howls against oppression, against poverty, against the deplorable and disgusting conditions in which the poor are forced to live and suffer in the industrialized world—only an academic critic could turn a sympathetic plea for justice for the poor into a vile, imperialist tract of American supremacy. When contemporary criticism stoops this low for the purposes of publication, we are chagrined. We are ashamed.

Biographies remain plentiful, and are steadily cranked out at an astonishing rate, the most recent being Alex Kershaw's *Jack London: A Life.* Jonathan Auerbach's *Male Call: Becoming Jack London*, when the author is not attempting literary criticism, is a brilliant study of London's self-marketing, his "becoming" the icon we know as Jack London. Auerbach treats London in the fashion we'd treat Sharon Stone or Quentin Tarrantino—as a celebrity bent on celebrity, and his book, though not literary criticism, is indisputably one of the best on London to date. Several volumes of critical "greatest hits" have been collected in addition to Cassuto's collection, most notably Ray Wilson's *Jack London: Essays in Criticism* and Jacqueline Tavernier-Courbin's *Critical Essays on Jack London.* Again, Professor Labor's extensive reviews of criticism cited above need not be restated.

A significant book, and perhaps the best written study of London's short fiction, is James I. McClintock's *Jack London's Strong Truths*, published originally in 1975 as *White Logic: Jack London's Short Stories*, and reprinted under the current title in 1997. As masterfully as I've seen anyone analyze the structural and narrative elements of short fiction, McClintock shows in his book that London, although he may have ended up not much more than a hack writer (note the "Smoke Bellew" stories—they're pale imitations of London's former self, much like the self-imitations produced by Hemingway and Faulkner near the ends of their careers), didn't set out to be a hack, rant as he might have about only writing for bucks.

London criticism is not plentiful, as a result of the second-rate status he has suffered in academic circles. Auerbach, in *Male Call*, sums up the criticism thusly:

> Put off, perhaps, by so open a striving for popularity, academic critics have for the most part not been very kind to Jack London, leaving the field to a relatively small band of loyalists. These keepers of the flame have tended to make their case somewhat defensively in three related ways: along conventional New Critical formalist lines; by way of various ideological analyses of London's thinking on now fashionable topics (race, class, gender), often with the goal of proving that London was not really such a racist or that he really did respect women despite his macho posturing; and/or, most pervasive, in terms of the brief but highly charged life that London led. Formalism and biography, we have been told, tend to be incompatible. But in the case of London studies, they have become mutually reinforcing, investing the scenes of London's life and analogous scenes he imagined in his writing with a special, reciprocal fascination, as if the fiction needed biographical glossing to continue to have currency.

As Auerbach contends, the criticism tends to be largely biographical in nature, scanning the fiction for elements which correspond with the "actual" events of London's life. This kind of treatment has played a factor in London's works being treated as if they are not literature, but artifact. We don't find the kind of studies of London's work that provide thoughtful analyses of the works *as literature*, as works *worthy of study*, as works from which we can learn about the nature of literature and aesthetics.

3

The two primary functions of literary criticism are to study an author's purpose, and to study an author's technique. More generally, we study ideas and linguistic delivery. This twofold focus of critical analysis goes as far back as Aristotle and continues today in myriad mutations and subdivisions. However, amid the din of increasing specialization in literary criticism, of increasing propensity to attempt scientifically oriented linguistic studies of literature, contemporary critics often tend to leap over intermediary steps, skipping over notions of style, for instance, and burrowing in with linguistic studies and semiotic analyses. This leads to a general neglect of some of the things that make literary artists different from commercial writers. For a semiotic or linguistic study of a literary writer more often than not produces results no more illuminating than similar studies of restaurant menus or billboard advertisements. Similarly, by focusing on content merely, and reducing content to social paradigms of correct thinking and incorrect thinking in terms of a given era's political climate, we run the risk of either elevating inferior works to lofty pedestals or condemning superior works to infernal depths. The reduction of literature to morphological units is an exercise for linguists, not critics. The study of literature in terms of politics is the proper area of sociology. The French writer E. M. Cioran writes:

> The real writer writes about beings, things, events, he does not write about writing, he uses words but does not linger over them, making them the object of his ruminations. He will be anything and everything ex-

cept an anatomist of the Word. Dissection of language is the fad of those who, having nothing to say, confine themselves to the saying.

Critics of late, however, have begun to think of themselves as writers, and books written by living and breathing men and women have become "texts" which are "written" as the "critic" (all readers are "critics") reads, the "critic" now the "author" of the "text" generated in the "mind" of the "critic." I was in a graduate course at the University of Houston when a professor, tenured twenty years before on a technicality and author of one book since his tenure-winning lawsuit—a book on Texas wines—scanned the room the first day of the course and began, "We writers."

Critics need to remember that they're not writers, a point James Tuttleton makes clearly and passionately in his essay "Some Modern Sophists." Tuttleton writes, concerning the recent trend of critics to elevate criticism not only to the level of primary creative art, but *higher* than creative art, "Claiming that the critic can be as creative as the poet is one way of getting revenge on the artist, who has often enough condemned the critic as a parasite, a bottom-feeder on original creation." In another essay, "The Griswold Effect," James L. Blewer writes:

> You see, the whole aim of being in an English department is not to enjoy literature but to destroy literature. I call this the Griswold Effect. Reverend Rufus Griswold, Edgar Allan Poe's literary executor, and who evidently harbored a secret resentment against Poe, purposefully botched the texts of Poe's work and sought to mitigate his importance by inventing wild stories about Poe's behavior. Griswold hated that Poe was a poet and that he, Griswold, was only a "literary

man" and anthologist of ladies' poetry. Most people I
know in English departments, both faculty and graduate students, have a similar hatred for the object of
their study, and spend their time not reading literature, or teaching people how to enjoy it, but stocking
up on theories, like bullets in their holster, with which
they can gun down great works of fiction, poetry, and
drama.

Blewer adds that critics have taken it upon themselves to
preach the gospel of criticism, of the critical act as the primary
act, the act which creates literature, since literature is nothing
more than a set of signifiers and signs which await the critic's
lordly and godlike breath to fill the works with life. A poem
by Ted Berrigan, "People of the Future," is telling here:

People of the future

while you are reading these poems, remember
you didn't write them,

I did.

Many modern critics may indeed be writing to get revenge
on the writers who have deemed them parasites, but literary
writers (and I use the word in the good old-fashioned sense of
the word, meaning people who have *written* creative works)
write for a variety of reasons, among them fame, a passion for
language, a yearning for immortality, the desire to alter the
course of society, a love of art. In order to achieve these various aims, writers hone their skills toward their various ends.
When assessing the value of an author and his work, it does
the discipline of literary criticism little service to superimpose
over a literary work *that which is not there*. When we superimpose Deconstruction Theory over a 19th-century text, we are

studying Deconstruction Theory, not the text itself. The same holds true for a great many current critical trends. It is largely for this reason that the arena of literary criticism has been marginalized in the past twenty years. Whereas, for instance, Leslie Fiedler's *Love and Death in the American Novel* remains in print in a trade paperback edition, being purchased by more than just graduate students of English and American literature, most contemporary critical studies remain published only by university presses and purchased only by libraries, professors of English, and their students. Lawrence's *Studies in Classic American Literature* remains, three generations after its original publication, in trade paper; most academic studies have only one very small university press run.

Criticism need not fade to a whimper. Much work remains to be done not only with Jack London but with the traditional canon and with the works that have been neglected by academia; there is critical work to be done which not only illuminates the work under study, but both literature as a function of society and literature in terms of itself.

The best criticism is that which teaches us not only something about the work under scrutiny, but something about ourselves.

The truly great writers, by definition, teach us something about ourselves. The truly great writers plumb their own souls and find that which is universal within. The best criticism is that which helps us to understand the great writers. The best criticism helps us to understand the universal truths underlying the work of the great and of the less than great but representative writers, and in this way, to understand our own variants of the universal truths.

If I do nothing else in this book, I hope to help the reader understand Jack London and his work just a little better.

III

OUT, OUT, OUT OF OAKLAND!

Oakland has produced two major writers.

It has produced Jack London.

And it has produced me.

And this is what every Oakland writer since London has thought, whether he announced it or not.

The Oakland of Jack London's youth was a deeply divided town, as it is now, the wealthy decisively segregated from the laboring poor. Until 1849, there was no Oakland; it was only after gold was discovered that Oakland became a desirable piece of real estate. Massive commercial expansion of San Francisco and the necessity for more shipping connections and docks and wharves in effect created Oakland. Originally owned by Don Luís María Peralta, the land which is now Oakland was stolen from Peralta by squatters in the wake of the Gold Rush of 1849. By the 1870s, with the exception of the area surrounding Lake Merritt and the downtown area, the Oakland basin was predominantly industrial, and the waterfront was deeded to Leland Stanford's Western Pacific Railroad in return for a transcontinental terminus. The entire waterfront of Oakland became an immense spread of railroad track, factories, loading docks, and wharves. This was where Jack London grew up.

John Perry, in his book *Jack London: An American Myth*, thinks Oakland was some kind of paradise. Mr. Perry attempts throughout his book to debunk the entire life of Jack London, claiming that London didn't know anything about sailing, that London didn't *really* have to work hard, that London was just a drunk, that London was a lame writer and a plagiarist. Perry goes through London's life's work and arrives at the conclusion that London was just a self-promoting liar. Perry writes of Oakland:

> Oakland—Jack London's home town, across the Bay? Locals called it "The Athens of America" and "Eden of the Pacific." Four daily newspapers existed in 1895, and the university boasted two thousand students that year. Three electric streetcar systems rolled between Oakland and Berkeley. One-time residents of this cultural city included Bret Harte, Henry George, Joaquin Miller, Gertrude Stein, and Robert Louis Stevenson. Karl Baedeker wrote in *The United States with an Excursion into Mexico, A Handbook for Travelers, 1893*: "The 'Brooklyn' of San Francisco is a flourishing city of 48,682 inhab., pleasantly situated on the E. shore of the Bay of San Francisco. It derives its name from the number of live-oaks in its streets and gardens. The value of its manufactures in 1890 was $6,335,000. The steam-railways which traverse Oakland convey passengers free of charge within the city limits."

In his zeal to prove London a liar, Perry cites a travel guide, which, of course, paints its destinations in rosy lights as a matter of course. Perry does not mention just who is doing the dirty work which produces the six million in manufacture— it's as if the products just create themselves in the middle of the industrial age. The "one-time inhabitants" are named, but not shown in their quarters, high in the mountains above

Oakland and its working poor. Robert Louis Stevenson only lived in the Bay Area for a couple of years, and Gertrude Stein got the hell out. As for Joaquin Miller, Joaquin Miller Park, on Skyline Boulevard is one of the biggest parks in the entire Bay Area; it used to be the grounds of Miller's Estate. Perry acts as if every person living in Oakland lived like Miller. Gertrude Stein once said of Oakland, "There is no there there." No *there* in this "cultural city."

I've heard Oakland called a lot of things, but a "cultural city" has never been one of them. Perry's attack on London is the kind of thing we'd expect to hear from the kind of critic who seems to be anything but lacking for funds. His research on his London attack took him to Rhode Island, Connecticut, England, Oregon, Ohio, California, Florida, Utah, Colorado, Iowa, Hawaii, British Columbia, New York, Minnesota, Pennsylvania, Massachusetts, Indiana, and dozens of universities. Anywhere looks pretty swell if you're rich. The poorest nation on the planet is a paradise if you're the overlord.

In his book *The California Progressives*, George E. Mowry describes turn-of-the-century California thusly:

> . . . notwithstanding the growing citrus culture, California was sparsely populated for its size and depended upon a traditional commercial, extractive, and agricultural economy. Far removed from other population and cultural centers of the country, its inhabitants felt their isolation. Writing at the start of the new century, Benjamin Ide Wheeler, president of the state university, described California as a backwater "where few people come except the very rich, and they only to stay a few months during the winter." The New York papers, he observed, never mentioned the state except to record "an earthquake, a murder, or a birth of a two-headed calf."

If the president of UC Berkeley is describing California as a backwater, we should find it curious that Mr. Perry finds Oakland to be a cultural Mecca.

A more accurate description than Perry's of Oakland specifically, through still provided by the upper crust, can be found in Georgia Loring Bamford's dainty biography, *The Mystery of Jack London*, published in 1931. Bamford was a contemporary of London's, a schoolmate first during the time London completed his high school education, and then at Berkeley during the year London studied there. She was a wealthy society lady, and her biography is a delicately written impressionistic account of her encounters with London, first as a classmate, and later in the parlor rooms of Oakland. Unlike Perry, whose agenda in his 1981 book is making London out to be a liar, Bamford *actually saw where London lived*, went to his neighborhood in West Oakland to take a look at how the other side lived, how the side not mentioned in the travel pamphlets drag themselves through life. She writes of the London family:

> They lived in an old "cottage," at what used to be called Brooklyn station near the shore of the Estuary. To form a judgment from the apparent condition of their close neighbors, it was what could only be called squalor of an aggravated type.
>
> Nearby there were scattered any number of "domiciles" of an indescribable ramshackle character. I have seen the London house, which was pointed out to me by a former neighbor, and as my memory serves me, it was a little better than the others; but not very much.
>
> Many of the shacks near by were built of wreckage; some from dismantled vessels, but most of them from old buildings, anything that would keep out the wind and the weather. Crevices were stuffed with old carpets and rags.

Of course, every element of modern sanitation was lacking. Such luxuries were not for poor people in those days.

This is Perry's "Eden of the Pacific."

Jack London's Oakland hasn't changed much since his time; it still creates and nurtures the passions and contradictions we find in Jack London's person and work. Oakland's not a town you willingly move to; it's a circle of hell from which you attempt to escape. In London's novel *The Valley of the Moon*, a thirteen-year-old boy named John says:

> Don't you sometimes feel you'd die if you didn't know what's beyond them hills an' what's beyond the other hills behind them hills? An' the Golden Gate! There's the Pacific Ocean beyond, and China an' Japan, an' India, an' . . . an' all the coral islands. You can go anywhere out through the Golden Gate—to Australia, to Africa, to the seal islands, to the North Pole, to Cape Horn. Why, all them places are just waitin' for me to come an' see 'em. I've lived in Oakland all my life, but I'm not going to live in Oakland the rest of my life, not by a long shot. I'm goin' to get away . . . away. . . .

But even if you do escape, you'll never get the stink out of your nose. Oakland is well known for being one of America's most violent cities, rife with racial tensions and a pulsing penchant toward Socialism that these days takes the form of a solid and unwavering left-wing vote.

Oakland—the home of both the Black Panthers and the site of the national headquarters of the Hell's Angels.

Oakland is a town I understand. It has rules that are clear, and in Oakland you don't sue people, as is the fashion when offended these sad days; you beat the hell out of them, or, better, you shame them. It is preferable to do both simultaneously. Sometimes you win the fight, sometimes you don't; but the point is that when the fight is finished, it's finished for good, and you go about your business and try not to cross paths again.

I'm not sentimental or nostalgic about Oakland, about a town that cheers louder for broken necks than for touchdowns—but at least the town has character. a blue-collar, shipyard beer-and-gin-and-whiskey-drinking character that is proud of being everything San Francisco is not.

Oaklanders build their cars from scratch, and they don't drink booze whose name they can't pronounce.

It's odd to me, the notions people from the South or the eastern seaboard have of California. Sure, I've seen people surf, but I'd wager they were more likely from Sheboygan, Wisconsin, than from Oakland. I've never surfed in my life, nor have I skied, nor have I skateboarded, nor have I ever known an Oaklander who did any of the above. My mother rode with the Hell's Angels in the sixties—their headquarters were cater-cornered to our backyard on 62nd Avenue—and, like Jack London, I was born a bastard and raised by a man who was not my father. Only when I became an adult did I discover I was without history, with a name that was not of my blood, in proper Oakland fashion.

It's not that uncommon for a fancy Easterner to come west, impress a young lady, inseminate her, and head on back. It's like slumming for whores in the ghetto for many East Coast men. They'll sleep with a lower-class California gal, but they won't marry her after they've knocked her up. What, after all, would the *people* back home, in *civilization*, think?

Jack London was born the bastard child of "Professor" W. H. Chaney, a lecturing "professional" astrologer who jammed right on out of town when Flora Wellman, Jack London's mother, announced she was pregnant. She blasted a hole through her head when he abandoned her, but was a lousy shot and lived. Chaney, a charmer, was from the sophisticated "East": if you're a Californian, anything on the other side of the Mississippi is the "East"—the concept of the "Midwest," a region puny to a Westerner and two-thousand miles away, is difficult to swallow. How could something nearer to New York than to Denver be considered the West? Native Californians have the impression that the East is a sprawl of class and sophistication, a land where everyone is educated except the Mafia thugs, a land where people still have lingering English accents leftover from their aristocratic ancestors in the British Isles. We don't really think about little towns in Connecticut, for instance, where the people have been inbreeding for 300 years and never exploring more than ten miles from their birthplaces. We can't conceive of Queens or New Jersey and their expanses of knuckleheads: isn't New Jersey where Princeton is? The East, we're led to believe, is the land of the landed and the educated. It's a land where people can recite their family trees back hundreds of years.

In California, we're lucky if we've met our grandparents, if anyone will admit who they are. There is some debate over London's birthright, as is predictable in the case of a bastard. However, his bastardy is a mere commonplace for an Oaklander. Most of the people I grew up with didn't know for sure who their fathers were. And plenty of the mothers weren't sure from whose sperm their children had sprung. Plenty of the fathers were Easterners who'd come West for military service, spent some merry time copulating with the local barbarians, and returned home to "civilization."

London was the "miscegenetic" spawn of a Yankee and Californian, and so was I. According to my mother (but who can be sure of these things? London's mother was trying to summon up the dead during seances, and my mother has 95 personalities, a Multiple Personality Disorder case), the reason I exist is that a boy from Connecticut, of French-Canadian Catholic ancestry, came to Oakland and slept with her when she was sixteen years old and knocked her up. When he found out she was pregnant, he told her he couldn't marry her because he was Catholic, and Catholics didn't marry pregnant girls. Besides, he came from a good family, and they wouldn't understand. She would never be accepted. That Yankee didn't know it, but he had created more than a bastard: he'd made a typical Oakland boy—hopeless, dreamless, bloodless—devoid of religion, culture, history, ethics, and family. He'd cut the umbilical cord and left me bloody on the pavement, but at the same time freed me from everything that binds being to humanity, child to family, clan to nation. Nourished on the piss and vomit of the gutter, on the sludge at the bottom of the human cesspool, I don't owe humanity a damn thing, and I have no hopes, no debts, no dreams.

And that's the way London feels, too. Born a bastard, reared in squalor, deprived of the opportunities of even an average person and condemned to serving the rich, London looks out on the world and sees what any impoverished Oakland boy sees: the corrupt and decadent and exploitative system of capitalist interests making animals out of the poor, bleeding the life out of them in corporate legal fashion. According to the historian George E. Mowry, at the beginning of the 1900s in California, one of the major power struggles

> centered around the rise of an increasingly politically conscious laboring class in urban California. But within the early years of the century the labor issue, while extremely important, was always secondary from the viewpoint of the entire state to the struggle to free the state from corporate rule. California, like so many of her sister commonwealths at the turn of the century,

had only the shadow of representative government, while the real substance of power resided largely in the Southern Pacific Railroad Company. To a degree perhaps unparalleled in the nation, the Southern Pacific and a web of associated economic interests ruled the state.

The state of California has since the days of the Gold Rush of '49 been a place where the workers have been trounced. Our literature—London, Steinbeck, Norris—is insistent on harping on the trouncing. The railroads, then the oil companies (Standard Oil primarily), the agricultural trusts—all have found unwary frontiersfolk Californians ripe for exploitation, especially during the late 19th century, when the state converted from wilderness to statehood and an industrial and shipping Mecca. First the American Indians, then the Spaniards, then the Mexicans, and then the working-class whites got the shaft: Native Californians have been getting it for 300 years now. We're feeling a bit raw.

Only those who *come* to California are hopeful, are dreamers. Their children, the true Californians, we bastard heaps of disenfranchised slag, have no such hopes. We are born at the edge of the world with radioactive water to the West and nuclear desert to the East. There's nowhere to go, and we have learned from our once-hopeful-now-failed parents that hope is for people better off than us. He'd done me a favor, that Yankee. He'd given me something that no Southerner, no Yankee, no Midwesterner can ever have truly—he'd given me the blessing of the Great Nothing.

Out of which I became an Oakland boy.

It's ironic that Clarice Stasz wrote a biography of Charmian and Jack London and called it *California Dreamers*; the term itself is oxymoronic. The title is evidence that her research revealed everything except the essence of the *true* Californian.

And she certainly didn't have a grip on the subspecies of
Californian: the Oaklander.

There are no California Dreamers.

The Oakland Raiders football team (their mascot a one-
eyed pirate—homage to Jack London's oyster pirate days)
is Oakland's primal symbol. The prized tickets for Raiders
games, when I was growing up, were those that lined the
area from which the opposing team emerged: people lined
up alongside the channel, and when the apes trotted out from
beneath the stands, over their heads the Raiders' fans poured
motor oil, beer cups full of piss, bags of dogshit, soiled baby
diapers. Jack Tatum, who once paralyzed a player with an especially effective tackle, was a local hero. The Raiders' train-
ing camp was within eyeshot of San Quentin, and the Raiders
actively recruited recent releases, boasting (we Oaklanders tell
people) more ex-cons than any other team in the NFL—or at
least that's what you read in *The Oakland Tribune.*

In a letter to Mabel Applegarth, dated November 30, 1898,
London writes, "If I knew that my life would be such, that I
was destined to live in Oakland, labor in Oakland at some
steady occupation, and die in Oakland—then to-morrow I
would cut my throat and call quits with the whole cursed
business."

Oakland is for the most part a festering ghetto, a filthy
grid of sagging wooden and cracking plaster houses that have
survived earthquakes but have not been repaired after the
earthquakes. From the elevated BART train, or from what
once was the Cypress Street double-decker portion of the
Nimitz Freeway before the '89 quake, you could see mile after
mile of war-zone poverty, overgrown yards littered with garbage and old rusted cars and discarded appliances, the homeless pushing shopping carts down the rubbled streets in sober
processions, prostitutes flashing their wares to any passer-by,

emaciated dogs dragging themselves along on their broken haunches, children running half naked through the alleys.

It's the town in which the man who raised me was raised, and his father before him. My great-grandfather, club-footed and slight of body, moved from Missouri to California in the wake of the gold rush and did not fare well. He wanted work in San Francisco, but ended up in Oakland, which, in and of itself, constitutes failure: Oakland is the town where people who can't make it in San Francisco live. Our family never fared well, working some of the nastiest jobs imaginable, my club-footed great-grandfather spreading tar on roads and rooftops, my grandfather as a jackhammer operator, my father as a tire-serviceman beating truck tires with a sledge hammer at a gas station, and my brother now following in his footsteps, swinging the same hammer. When I was young, we lived in a welfare project on Cypress Street, not three miles from Jack London Square. We moved out of the projects when my father got a job at a Texaco gas station—he bought a 19-foot trailer and parked it next to the station, and there my father, two brothers, and I lived until a rich person (a rich person was anyone who owned a house), who had an account at the gas station, reported us to the City of Oakland, which cited my father for unfit living conditions (we had to empty the toilet's holding tank, one bucket at a time, into the gas station toilet). After that, the three of us boys, 8, 10, and 12, had to get jobs to help pay the rent. One of us was a paperboy, another sold marijuana, and the other stole television sets.

In Oakland, either you are rich, living around Lake Merritt or in the Piedmont hills, or you are a wage worker, performing the dirty work for the rich, fixing their cars and their roads and building houses you can't afford to buy.

And the poor of Oakland truly hate the rich. The rich of California are conspicuous consumers of the vilest and most distasteful variety, and have been for a hundred years. Whereas, for instance, Old Money New Yorkers are conspicuously inconspicuous, walking their dogs in Gramercy Park wearing sweatpants and t-shirts, there are no Old Money Californians, not in the sense that money passed down has brought with it a semblance of culture and manners and decorum. The New Money gang has no mercy whatsoever on the poor they exploit, and never has. "A Chicago millionaire who wanted to gain social recognition built a college," notes Richard O'Connor, "but when a San Franciscan gets to be immensely wealthy he builds a palace of a stable with marble halls, Brussels carpets and hot and cold water in every stall." Riots frequently marched into the neighborhoods of the rich of San Francisco, and in Oakland, the rich moved to the Oakland Hills to fortress themselves from insurgencies. The Bay Area was during London's time rife with class hatred as a result of the conspicuous consumption of the rich. O'Connor writes:

> The most striking thing about San Francisco in those several years before London was born—and after it, for that matter—was the contrast between the very rich on Nob Hill and the "work beasts," as London was to call them, in the wooden-frame tenements terraced below. "The 1870's had brought a new silver splendor to San Francisco," as the city's social historian Julia Cooley Altrocchi has written, "overlaying its earlier gold, yielding more resplendent houses, costumes, jewels, manners, displays, entertainments." But underneath this gorgeous silver-plating there were grimy layers of resentment and class hatred. Even Gilded Age New York couldn't outdo San Francisco in the matter of excess.

The excess of the flashy nouveau rich did not escape London any more than it escapes the ghetto-dwellers in Oakland today. The young Jack London despised the rich, and would have had them dead. His high-school classmate Georgia Bamford notes that at the Christmas Assembly at the end of the semester, London gave a speech, and

> [b]efore people knew it their ears were being assailed by the most truculent Socialistic diatribe that I have ever heard. He was ready to destroy society and civilization; to break down all resistance with any force and commit the most scientific atrocities. He even suggested the Guillotine as desirable.

Perhaps because of the many waves of instantaneous wealth that have washed over California over the past 150 years—the California gold rush, the Nevada silver lode, the Yukon gold rush, Southern California oil discoveries, the mechanization of agricultural methods in the Central Valley, Hollywood's movie industry, the post WWII defense industry, the computer boom of Silicon Valley—the nouveau rich have always had contempt for the working class; for the working class consists of those who, for generations, have failed.

When I was in high school in East Oakland, once or twice a year the rich kids from the high school in the hills came to our school in their Porsches and BMWs and Jaguars and they destroyed our cars—junkyard heaps we had repaired into barely running condition—smashing our windshields and slashing our tires and spray-painting their school logo over the paint-jobs of our twenty-year-old Ramblers, Falcons, Galaxies, and Polaras. In retaliation, we stalked them at their local hangouts, late, and with baseball bats and tire-irons evened the score—not on their cars, but on their bones. Nothing ever happened to the rich kids for destroying our cars. We, on the other hand, went to juvenile hall.

John, in *The Valley of the Moon*, says, "We're the white folks an' the children of white folks, that was too busy being good to be smart. We're the white folks that lost out."

And the black folks have lost out in Oakland, too. In *The Second Gold Rush: Oakland and the East Bay in World War II*, Marilynn S. Johnson details the buildup of Oakland during WWII. Oakland, along with Long Beach, Portland, and Seattle, became a major city because of the shipbuilding industry, and anyone who could work was employed. Bums were hired from beneath bridges, hoboes were hired off of boxcars. When these folk ran out, the Kaiser Company, according to Johnson, recruited from far and wide, including blacks from the South. The story my grandfather told me about the arrival of the blacks is a bit different, and more telling. One afternoon, standing on the porch of his house, my grandfather showed me a bullet hole in the wood. "A colored boy was shot on the porch," he said. "He was in a gunfight right here on my porch." He closed his eyes and shook his head. "I'm glad your grandmother wasn't here to see what has happened to this town." He then told me about how Oakland used to be in the days of the streetcars, in the days when people talked to each other on the streets, in the days when a person could walk to the store and back. He told me that the reason the colored folks were so angry is that Kaiser sent out flyers throughout the South to all the predominantly black areas, and on the flyers it said that anyone who wanted a good job only needed to get on the trains that would be coming through. Kaiser sent trains through the South, and brought trainload after trainload of blacks to Oakland, where he put them to work at jobs in the ship building industry. They worked, they were paid well, they bought houses, they brought their extended families up from the South, they settled.

Then the war ended, and Kaiser fired them all. No more Victory Ships were needed. The black people who'd been living respectable lives, paying mortgages, buying cars, now found themselves unemployed, homeless, and uneducated in a town that had never before had a black population of significance. According to Johnson, at the onset of the war, in 1940, blacks constituted less than 10% of the total population of the East Bay. By 1950, blacks were about 47% of the total population. Johnson cites a federal agent who supplies a description of the kinds of homes blacks found themselves occupying:

> There were at least 6 instances where clusters of shacks were so horrible that the only possible solution would be to remove their occupants immediately and burn the shacks. . . . One of these groups was housed in a chicken house, entirely without windows. . . . This room housed a shipyard welder, his wife, and 5 children. Three of the children sleep on a thin concrete floor less than 20 feet from the muddy banks of the San Pablo Creek with drainage from a privy and a garbage pile toward the house rather than toward the creek.

Through nothing more than a desire to better their lives, the blacks found themselves unemployed, uneducated, and despised by the white, Mexican, and Asian populations. And they were pissed. Their children were my classmates in the public schools.

It's not surprising that, early on, many of us—black, white, Mexican (considered aliens even today in a land that is historically their own), and Asian (the children and grandchildren of people locked up in the Mojave desert in "relocation centers," the wartime euphemism for concentration camps, FDR's version of Bush's Guantanamo)—ended up socialists—if not anarchists—without knowing what a socialist or anarchist was, cheering when the Oakland Fires raged through the hilltop mansions, when mudslides dragged the fancy houses down to our part of town, when some rich dude got carjacked and murdered while cruising for a whore on San Pablo Boulevard. We pumped gas for the rich, we mopped their offices, we mowed their lawns, and we unplugged their toilets. In our homes, the homes of the workers, there were newspapers, copies of *Sports Illustrated*, trade magazines, and the works of Jack London.

Jack London's story is not as uncommon as one would think. When one escapes from Oakland, one's feelings toward the place and the people become confused. Someone who escapes from the hell which is Oakland cannot help but feeling superior to all those who remain in its sewer. "If I did it, so can they," an escapee would say. "And if they haven't escaped as I have, it's because they haven't worked as hard as I have, or because they are somehow inherently inferior. Either way, it's their own fault. Let 'em rot." At the same time, however, an escapee feels rage at the indignities the rich seem to impose, by their very existence, on the poor; and the escapee feels the need, almost maniacal in nature, to burn down the fortresses of those in power. The man who has escaped Oakland's ghettos, at the same time as being disgusted by what London, in "These Bones Shall Rise Again," calls "the mob-minded mass," feels a kinship with the poor, a sympathy for their wretched condition, and an understanding that, given slightly different circumstances, he could have remained one of them. Bloom, in *The Western Canon*, writes:

> The freedom to be an artist, or a critic, necessarily rises out of social conflict. But the source or origin of the freedom to perceive, while hardly irrelevant to

aesthetic value, is not identical with it. There is always guilt in achieved individuality; it is a version of the guilt of being a survivor and is not productive of aesthetic value.

London's wavering back and forth between his hatred of the poor and his sponsorship of the poor is a version of "survivor guilt": but it's a survivor guilt that is produced not by accident, but by his own will to escape his roots.

We Oaklanders know who we are, and we know what we want, and what we want is OUT. We want out, out, *out of Oakland*. Carolyn Johnston writes, concerning London's conversion to socialism after tramping around the country, that

> his conversion to socialism did not change him fundamentally, but it helped him articulate his own experience of class struggle and set into motion a conflict which he tried unsuccessfully to resolve throughout the rest of his life. The image of the wolf symbolized his dilemma: how to rise out of the working class and still join with it in hastening the revolution. He wanted to be a self-sufficient lone wolf, raging against the forces of nature and ruthlessly fighting for survival. At the same time, he was the wolf in a pack, needing comradeship in order to survive as he had during his escapades as a seal hunter. Of course, London preferred to be the leader of the pack. He claimed that his genuine comrades were workers and maintained that "it was the proletarian side of his life that he revered the most and to which he would cling as long as he lived." His experiences with material and emotional deprivation made him identify with the suffering of the working class. Although he genuinely sympathized with the oppressed workers, London's strongest ambition was to escape the working class himself.

She's pretty close here: London wants *out*. He wants to escape the working class, for the fall from the bourgeoisie downward does not carry the ramifications of the fall from the working class. If one falls from the bourgeois, one ends up flipping pizzas for a living. If one falls from flipping pizzas, one is doomed. But what Johnston doesn't quite understand in her book is that London not only "genuinely sympathized with the oppressed workers," but considered, truly thought himself to be one of them.

Many critics and biographers have taken London to task, calling London an armchair Socialist, saying he never had an iota of sympathy for the poor but, rather, used a feigned sympathy for the poor as a means of achieving a large readership. But Bamford's firsthand account of London giving one his speeches on Socialism seems to refute this:

> But beneath all his literary ambition that showed on the surface, he was at heart, mind, and body, a socialist. His blood was full of it. Boiling with it. His street speaking proved this, and the violence of his remarks that I have heard was terrifying in the extreme. When giving one of these talks he seemed to lose himself and to be clutching at the throats of his enemies in "The class struggle." His vigor and earnestness showed Ambition, but in the background there loomed the hideous red devil of Revenge—revenge for some fancied wrong.

He always saw himself as the boy from Oakland he uses in *The Valley of the Moon*, the boy who says, "I'm not going to live in Oakland the rest of my life." London's description in "The Tramp" of the East Enders of London reads like a description of the folks of my neighborhood in Oakland:

> Here humanity rots. . . . Or, as a legislative report puts it: "Here infantile life unfolds its bud, but perishes

before its first anniversary. Here youth is ugly with loathsome disease, and the deformities which follow physical degeneration."

These are the men and women who are what they are because they were not better born, or because they happened to be unluckily born in time and space. Gauged by the needs of the system, they are weak and worthless. The hospital and the pauper's grave await them, and they offer no encouragement to the mediocre worker who has failed higher up in the industrial structure. Such a worker, conscious that he has failed, conscious from the hard fact that he cannot obtain work in the higher employments, finds several courses open to him. He may come down and be a beast in the social pit, for instance; but if he be of a certain caliber, the effect of the social pit will be to discourage him from work. In his blood a rebellion will quicken, and he will elect to become either a felon or a tramp.

We know what we are, and we know what we're likely to become. We can stand on our tar-paper rooftops and see the shimmer of San Francisco to the West, and we can turn about and see the tree-shrouded palazzos gate-guarded and nestled in the Oakland Hills. And we know how the buildings got built, how the houses get cleaned. And we hate the sons of bitches for whom we labor.

Unless we become the sons of bitches for whom other people work. Then we're not quite sure just who to hate. We're not sure if we should just enjoy the good life, or if we should lead our relatives and friends to revolt. London again, in "The Class Struggle":

It has been shown, theoretically and actually, that there is a class struggle in the United States. The quarrel over the division of the joint product is irreconcilable. The

> working class is no longer losing its strongest and most
> capable members. These men, denied room for their
> ambition in the capitalist ranks, remain to be the lead-
> ers of the workers, to spur them to discontent, to make
> them conscious of their class, to lead them to revolt.

We grow up hearing from our parents, our grandparents, our
neighbors, the local shopkeepers, that we are those "denied
room" for our ambitions. We see the proof of this all around
us: friends, family, neighbors ruined by lawyers and business-
men and real-estate moguls and congressmen and ex-wives.

We see hard-working, honest folk ruined and beaten into
shapeless, unrecognizable heaps of fallen humanity. Sometimes, though—just sometimes—someone gets out. Of my
high school class of over 400, 205 graduated, and five went
on to college. Dozens died before hitting their eighteenth
birthdays. More than I can count simply disappeared.

We are the mediocre, and we know it, and, as London says
in "The Tramp":

> For the mediocre there is no hope. Mediocrity is a
> sin. Poverty is the penalty of failure,—poverty, from
> whose loins spring the criminal and the tramp, both
> failures, both discouraged workers. Poverty is the in-
> ferno where ignorance festers and vice corrodes, and
> where the physical, mental, and moral parts of nature
> are aborted and denied.

But what if we escape? What if we end up in those hills looking down on the cesspool stewing and rotting and sinking
into East Bay mud?

Well, instead of making up our minds to go one way or the
other, instead of deciding "To hell with the poor" or "Viva la
revolution!"—instead of embracing one and only one of these
views, we stand behind both.

Most of us don't try to work out this philosophical opposition.

Jack London tries. He tries in his short stories and essays and novels. But he never arrives at a solution, not a human solution.

The closest he comes is *The Call of the Wild*.

The hero is a half-breed mutt. A dog.

IV

THE NORTHLAND

In 1905 London ran for Mayor of Oakland. He got 981 votes. Oakland, clearly, didn't want him.

He had already chosen not to champion Oakland, though, not to stake his literary claim on the shores of the bay.

Our greatest writers have mapped out territories for themselves. Hawthorne's New England, Melville's Pacific Ocean, Hemingway's Paris and Spain, Faulkner's postage stamp of earth, Twain's Mississippi River Valley, Flannery O'Connor's Georgia, Sherwood Anderson's Ohio, Cormac McCarthy's Texas/Mexico border. It seems a characteristic of American writers to stake a claim in a plot of land and mine it for all it's worth. We're still acting like settlers in a new land, searching for our own strike, homesteading the literary terrain.

Notice that with the exception of Melville, these writers all lived significant portions of their lives in the area about which they wrote. Their use of the territory has more to do with their own geographical location than anything else, it would seem. That they elevated their home turf into mythological proportions, that they saw their respective terrains as microcosms of the world at large, doesn't speak to the regions specifically. Had Flannery O'Connor lived in Montana instead of Georgia, she most likely would have turned Montana into a mythic region. Faulkner, had he lived in a rural Pennsylvania town, would have transformed that town into myth and legend, and we'd have had Amish families instead of Baptists. Melville, however, spent only a short period of his life on the sea, and then mythologized it, searching for something huge in order to make the leap from metaphor to metaphysics.

Likewise, Jack London, who spent the better part of his life in Oakland, chooses not to map the actual terrain of Oakland, but instead transliterates his social ideas, generated by his Oaklander experience, into his Northland, his Yukon and Alaska, choosing to utilize perhaps the most vast of any terrain to which an American has yet laid claim. Though Melville has claimed the sea, it's likely that no American writer will ever claim as big a piece of dirt as London. The forbidding nature of the North, the still mysterious nature of the frozen wastes (the subject still of science fiction), will remain mythological until mankind figures out a way to alter the earth's axis.

The writers whose terrains have been unfamiliar, mysterious, murky, and clouded with a threatening and foreboding mystique have made no bones about using the nature of their landscapes to great, and usually mythic, effects. Melville's vast oceans stretch out like watery tundra; Faulkner's dark swamps baffle and breathe death and life and timeless expanses of blood; O'Connor's Georgian forests and farms and small towns operate as microcosms of the nation as a whole and smack of things we know and yet know not; Hawthorne's New England rattles our bones with the ghosts of our collective national pasts. In all these mythic regions, the swell and pulse of humanity at large is represented in microcosm. Yet only a few of these—Melville's seas, Solzhenitsyn's Siberia, García Márquez's jungles, London's Northland—by their very nature evoke metaphysics and the spirit and the full weight of man and his place in the cosmos. James I. McClintock in *Jack London's Strong Truths*, writes that London's Northland is the unchartered land of the spirit where man seeks his identity by facing death, by participating in life's essential contest for preservation of meaningful selfhood. It is not merely the place to escape from civilization; instead, it is the place where men could confront the disturbing natural facts of life (actuality) and undertake a romantic quest for identity (ideals). The Alaskan landscape, the cosmic landscape, is identified with a naturalistic logic that denies human significance. This is startling because London sees the frontier unlike any writer who preceded him. Hamlin Garland in his short stories, for instance, had his characters withdraw from civilization to find new identities only to be disappointed by the dreary facts of the middle-border; but no one, until London, had put this confrontation in such darkly dramatic and universal terms.

I've been to Alaska in the dead of winter. I made the more-common-than-is-known trek to Alaska when I graduated from high school and worked on the Alaska Pipeline, worked on fishing boats and in canneries. The Alaska experience is a rite of passage for many of the poor in Oakland—hard work coupled with the reward so seldom seen in the lower classes: good pay. A sturdy 18-year-old could make, at the time I graduated from high school in 1979, upwards of $1500 per 84-hour work week, and that much cash back then was a fortune—minimum wage was two-and-a-half bucks an hour, and my friends that stayed in Oakland were taking home $86 bucks for a 40-hour work week schlogging away at jobs like scrubbing the smoke off the furniture recovered from burned out houses.

The chemicals they used burned the skin right off their hands.

Alaska, though—Alaska was our gold field, and the local papers, every May, would advertise the jobs just waiting for us. I've seen the sun slip across the southern horizon between 11:30 in the morning and 12:30 in the afternoon: it looks like a frozen peppermint disk. The air is so cold at 70 degrees below zero, or, as London would put it, with 102 degrees of frost, that your lungs hurt when you inhale. When you walk indoors from outside, the frozen air you'd been breathing, you find, has caked on your face in sheets of ice, and the ice slips down your face like rivers of snot melting in the warmth of furnace and stove. And there's a difference between 40 below and 70 below—you can feel it in your bones. 40 below is cross-country skiing weather; at 70 below, you just stay inside and wait. Ravens sit in the street as big as dogs, waiting for animal—or man—to freeze to death and supply dinner. Eskimos, drunk, stagger out of the bars of Fairbanks and pass out in the snow on their way home: their bodies are found during the Spring thaw when the river cracks free and begins again to flow. The citizens kill their limits of game every year, and they display the skins and horns in their bare-log living rooms. Dog piss from mush-team kennels freezes on the trees like the wax of melting candles. When you spit, you hear it crack into an ice-gob before it hits the snow. When you're in a place like this, you are aware constantly of your own puniness, of how very little man matters, of how one stupid move—a step on thin ice, a drunken stagger, a wet pair of shoes—can get you dead.

The "White Silence" London writes about is a very real thing.

London, in the opening pages of *White Fang*, writes:

> A vast silence reigned over the land. The land itself was
> a desolation, lifeless, without movement, so lone and

cold that the spirit of it was not even that of sadness. There was a hint in it of laughter, but of a laughter more terrible than any sadness—a laughter that was mirthless as the smile of the Sphinx, a laughter cold as the frost and partaking of the grimness of infallibility. It was the masterful and incommunicable wisdom of eternity laughing at the futility of life and the effort of life.

The White Silence is a god, a force from the heavens that presses down upon a man, that rises from underfoot. It is a god which whispers a chant in your ear, *Memento mori*—Remember, you must die. In Faulkner's swamps, if you stop moving, if you just stand there, nature will either eat you or suck you down into the mud and consume you like Sutpen's rotting house. In London's Northland, if you stop moving in the summer you'll be eaten alive. In the winter, you'll be frozen hard as a TV-dinner burrito. As described in *White Fang*, the Northland is no city rigged with social programs to help out the weak:

> On the sled, in the box, lay a third man whose toil was over,—a man whom the Wild had conquered and beaten down until he would never move nor struggle again. It is not the way of the Wild to like movement. Life is an offence to it, for life is movement; and the Wild aims always to destroy movement. . . . and most ferociously and terribly of all does the Wild harry and crush into submission man—man, who is the most restless of life, ever in revolt against the dictum that all movement must in the end come to the cessation of movement.

Existence is antithetical to the intention of the cosmos, a cosmos which is bent on the destruction of the weak, the feeble, and the stupid.

London's Northland is a testing ground on which man is capable of discovering himself and his relationship to the cosmos, to his god. In Conrad's *Heart of Darkness*, Marlow makes an analogous journey into a primordial land—the jungles of Africa. In those jungles,

> [t]here were moments when one's past came back to one, as it will sometimes when you have not a moment to spare to yourself; but it came in the shape of an unrestful and noisy dream, remembered with wonder amongst the overwhelming realities of this strange world of plants, and water, and silence. And this stillness of life did not in the least resemble a peace. It was the stillness of an implacable force brooding over an inscrutable intention. It looked at you with a vengeful aspect.

Like Conrad's jungles in *Heart of Darkness*, in which Marlow is forced to confront a primordial silence which is godlike and animated, "an implacable force brooding over an inscrutable intention" and "vengeful," London's Northland in *White Fang* shimmers with dark spirits:

> On every side was the silence, pressing upon them with a tangible presence. It affected their minds as the many atmospheres of deep water affect the body of the diver. It crushed them with the weight of unending vastness and unalterable decree. It crushed them into the remotest recesses of their own minds, pressing out of them, like juices from the grape, all the false ardors and exaltations and undue self-values of the human soul, until they perceived themselves finite and small, specks and motes, moving with weak cunning and little wisdom amidst the play and interplay of the great blind elements and forces.

It makes sense that London was creating a godlike force out of his Northland. America in London's time, as now, needed something to fill its existential void.

A nation come of age during revolutionary times, during the sloughing-off of institutionalized religion and the prevailing Christianity of the preceding thousand years, America ever seeks something to fill the gap left by the symbolic execution of God with the beheading of Louis XVI during the French Revolution. The death of God is the birth of godless metaphysics, and the writers we consider to be our great spokespeople, our canon of literary saints, are a group of writers who have either attempted to define a new metaphysics to fill the existential vacuum left by the death of God, writers like Emerson, Dickinson, Whitman, Thoreau, and London, or writers who have rued and/or ridiculed the absence of a definable metaphysical system, such as Hemingway, Chopin, Melville, Pynchon, Eliot, Donald Barthelme, and Cormac McCarthy. America's literary history is the record of the struggle to deal with the absence of a *purpose*, the absence of a *raison d'être* in a godless world. Even in today's movies we find this search dramatized: film after film presenting worlds which strip away society and show mankind in post-apocalyptic testing zones—*Mad Max* and a post-nuclear world, *Waterworld* and an earth without land, the *Terminator* films and their world of machine domination, *The Planet of the Apes* and a world in which humanity is knocked back down the evolutionary ladder.

London, like Twain and Cooper before him, removes his characters from the drawing rooms of Europe and sends them into nature—in London's case, to the wilderness of the Northland, and the rules, away from the paradigms of formal society, are left for London to derive from nature and from his characters' own souls. London works toward his own metaphysical system, and in order to develop that system, he must get man alone and by himself in the vastness of a brutal and indifferent cosmos.

Part of the perennial appeal of London is that he is able to show us what we are when we are in solitude, for it is only in solitude that we discover that thing we sometimes call God. In his story "The White Silence," London writes:

> Nature has many tricks wherewith she convinces man of his finity,—the ceaseless flow of the tides, the fury of the storm, the shock of the earthquake, the long roll of heaven's artillery,—but the most tremendous, the most stupefying of all, is the passive phase of the White Silence. All movement ceases, the sky clears, the heavens are as brass; the slightest whisper seems sacrilege, and man becomes timid, affrighted at the sound of his own voice. Sole speck of life journeying across the ghostly wastes of a dead world, he trembles at his audacity, realizes that his is a maggot's life, nothing more. Strange thoughts arise unsummoned, and the mystery of all things strives for utterance. And the fear of death, of God, of the universe, comes over him,—the hope of the Resurrection and the Life, the yearning for immortality, the vain striving of the imprisoned essence,—it is then, if ever, man walks alone with God.

In America today, the notion of solitude is a fading thing, and we grow ever more godless. As the communications era develops, we are increasingly unable to ever sense our solitary personalities. The work of Jane Austen and Henry James has come back into vogue, and is being canvassed for film possibilities—we're in an era that would much rather know about how people interact socially than how people behave when they're in isolation. James and Austen are concerned with the nuances of proper behavior, of social repercussions, of the fine distinctions between correct and incorrect, between the proper way to part one's hair and the improper way.

We're in an era now that doesn't much want to consider Man Alone. We are defined in terms of our relationship to society, and even infants are now required to have social security numbers. What we are becomes increasingly difficult to ascertain. But what we are is beasts. London writes, in his essay "The Somnambulists":

> Chained in the circle of his own imaginings, man is only too keen to forget his origin and to shame that flesh of his that bleeds like all flesh and that is good to eat. Civilization (which is part of the circle of his imaginings) has spread a veneer over the surface of the soft-shelled animal known as man. It is a very thin veneer; but so wonderfully is man constituted that he squirms on his bit of achievement and believes he is garbed in armor-plate.
>
> Yet man to-day is the same man that drank from his enemy's skull in the dark German forests, that sacked cities, and stole his women from neighboring clans like any howling aborigine. The flesh-and-blood body of man has not changed in the last several thousand years. Nor has his mind changed.

Marlow, in *Heart of Darkness*, concurs, and when watching the savages on shore says:

> "The earth seemed unearthly. We are accustomed to look upon the shackled form of a conquered monster, but there—there you could look at a thing monstrous and free. It was unearthly, and the men were—No, they were not inhuman. Well, you know, that was the worst of it—this suspicion of their not being inhuman. . . . what thrilled you was just the thought of their

> humanity—like yours—the thought of your remote
> kinship with this wild and passionate uproar. Ugly."

It's not that we have changed, if London and Conrad are correct, but that we have managed to shield ourselves from ourselves, that we have figured out ways to avoid our inner selves,
that we have constructed society in such a manner that we do
not have to deal with the remote tinglings of our animality.
When we are offended, we do not strike out with a fist—there
are laws to prevent us from this animal behavior. No, instead
we sue the offender and ruin his life, get him fired from his
job, take all the money he has worked for, send him to the
poorhouse. Our ability to shield ourselves from solitude has
increased to such a point that by law in this country we cannot exist outside of society. We're that afraid.

We don't know who we are, and we generally don't want
to know. We don't want to know what beasts we really are,
and we don't want to know what we'd do if we were in a situation like that of the Donner Party snowed in for the winter
on the roof of the Sierras.

Jack London wants us to know.

He wants us to know our primordial selves.

He wants us to see that we are indeed alone, and that the
flimsy illusion we've created for ourselves called "civilization"
is bogus and reduces us rather than elevates us. James Mc-
Clintock writes:

> Rather than portraying characters who master them-
> selves and their environments, London depicted them
> either reaching an uneasy accommodation with inter-
> nal and external forces or being destroyed by them. In
> the best stories in *The Son of the Wolf* and the following
> collections, indifferent or even sadistically irrational
> forces inhibit man's puny efforts to control his fate:

they are not man-oriented or man-controlled. Rather than nineteenth century preoccupations, London engaged twentieth century concerns: alienation, disenchantment, ironic ambivalence, and impotence.

London's appeal is universal because try as we might to convince ourselves that we are otherwise, we are creatures of the flesh, subject to the whims of nature and circumstance. Our alienation is eternal, and if we're not feeling alienated, it's probably because we're stoned on the comforts of this great land of gluttony. London plucks a universal string because he is concerned with the primordial condition of man's isolation, an isolation that is shared by all humanity whether in a metropolis or on a pot farm in Kentucky.

When we think of the great characters of literature, we usually come up with a list of outcasts, misfits, and solitary souls. Ahab, Lear, Robinson Crusoe, Kurtz, Hamlet, Huck Finn, Shylock, Gatsby, Yossarian, Quixote, Natty Bumppo, Hester Prynne, Sutpen, Poldy Bloom, Hurstwood, Moll Flanders. We don't usually cite among the list of great characters folks like Lambert Strether or Becky Sharp.

The solitary nature of our heroes more often than not leads to what we call adventure.

We call London an "adventure" writer—and we do this with a snideness that is usually reserved for folks like Danielle Steele and Stephen King; but adventure has always been the stuff of literature. During his time, London was writing the equivalent of the "minority" literature today: Toni Morrison's downtrodden black ghetto-dwellers are hard to distinguish from London's East Enders, and there's only a fine line between the hero of Ellison's Invisible Man and London the Boy Socialist. The ghetto "adventure" is the stuff of countless movies, of countless studies, of much of the literature which

constitutes the field of African-American Studies. In London's
time, and, though rarely acknowledged, now as well, the "submerged tenth," as London called it, was largely Catholic and
significantly Caucasian, alien to the literate culture and sor-
didly exotic—the true stuff of literature. For adventure of the
finest order is this: a quest or a battle. The quest of Odysseus
or the battle of Achilles. Both are searches for the meaning of
the self amid the din of society.

Popular literature, rather than posing the painful questions which deal with man's place in the cosmos, reinforces
the position that the people of the respective time would like
to think themselves occupying. Earle Labor has done us the
favor of examining the popular literature of London's day,
and writes, in *Jack London*:

> Because we have been conditioned by more than three
> generations of Realism, it is difficult to imagine the
> kind of fiction that dominated American magazines at
> the turn of the century. Perhaps the easiest way is to
> look at a few issues of the prestigious *Atlantic Monthly*.
> Volumes 84 and 85 (1899 and 1900) disclose a genuine
> editorial concern for social and political relevance in
> the publication of such articles as Jacob A. Riis's series
> on the slums, Frank Norris's "Comida: An Experience
> in Famine" (an essay on the civilian war victims in
> Cuba), William James's *Talks to Teachers on Psychol-
> ogy*, and Prince Peter Kropotkin's *Autobiography of a
> Revolutionist*. But the fiction in these volumes scarcely
> suggests such concern. For example, Mary Johnston's
> *To Have and to Hold*—a serialized historical romance
> reported to have doubled *Atlantic Monthly*'s circulation
> in 1900—is set in early seventeenth-century Virginia;
> the action revolves about the love affair of Captain
> Ralph Percy and the lovely Jocelyn Leigh as they en-
> dure the tribulations of piracy, Indian savagery, and

Lord Carnal's lecherous villainy. . . .

If William Dean Howells's teacup therapy had not managed to rid the popular novel of such sugar-and-spice Romanticism, the short story—virtually ignored in Realist theory—was worse yet. In the August 1899 issue of the *Atlantic Monthly*, for instance, Elizabeth Stuart Phelps's "Loveliness: A Story" begins typically: "Loveliness sat on an eider-down cushion embroidered with cherry-colored puppies on a pearl satin cover. . . . For Loveliness was a little dog... the essence of tenderness; set, soul and body, to one only tune. To love and be beloved—that was his life." And, in the January 1900 issue, Margaret I. Knapp's "Mother" ends just as typically: "Jack, dear heart, it was selfish in me to . . . leave you; but I had to do it,—I had to see my mother. Mother knows."

Such samples, culled from America's foremost literary magazine, help to explain why the period has been called the Mauve Decade. . . . Into this literary hothouse Jack London entered as a bracing draft of Arctic air.

London was a departure from the East's sissified stronghold on letters. He was a "token" poor-boy. He was in effect and for all practical purposes, a minority writer. And in America, we have a history of "minority" writers, writers who write not of the norm, but of the hidden subculture of the nation, becoming the focus of our literature and culture. Witness the popularity in film of gangsters and ghetto-dwelling monsters: we are endlessly fascinated by our nation's dirty underbelly.

We're fascinated by our scum.

Because we fear, if not know, that our scum reflects what we just might be when we strip away our titles, our names, our degrees, our social safety nets.

When the dust settles we'll not find Updike, Phillip Roth, Cheever, and Joyce Carol Oates heading up the list of the great 20th-century American authors; thankfully, they will be gone forever. And when African-American authors have become firmly entrenched in the canon, and not just as "African-American Authors," we'll find them right alongside London, whose racism is no more pronounced than that of Alice Walker.

Minority writers—and I use the word "minority" not in the sense of melanin level but rather in the sense of writers who operate outside the mainstream of society for whatever reason—have tended, during the past two centuries, toward examinations of either social problems or matters of existential purport. Outside of the flow of society, the writers tend either to critique that society to which they only marginally belong, noting its qualities and problems with distant scrutinizing eyes, or just as commonly they collapse inward, charting the landscape of their own alienation. Jonathan Harold Spinner, in his essay "Jack London's *Martin Eden*: The Development of the Existential Hero," makes he following observations:

> The modern existential dilemma, that overworked phrase, can be defined as the loss of identity, the feeling of alienation, the lack of faith so well-documented in so much of modern literature. A child of the industrial and scientific revolutions, one of its first propounders was Thomas Carlyle, in his book *Sartor Resartus*. This is one of the first modern works that carefully documents the loss of faith in an orderly universe because of the pressures of the industrial and scientific revolutions. Although the existential dilemma was hidden for three-quarters of a century in America behind the twin facades of the westering myth and the Horatio Alger legend, the myths of escape and success, *Martin Eden* breaks through as one of the first fictional statements of American existentialism.

Granted, much of this is puffed-up marketing for his subject matter, Spinner bordering on the preposterous when claiming that *Martin Eden* is one of the "first fictional statements of American existentialism," given the precursors of Cooper, Melville, Hawthorne, Emerson, Thoreau, Twain, Whitman, Dickinson, and nearly every other important American writer since the Puritans, but what's useful is this: Spinner notes one of the most important aspects of London's work—London's existentialism. This existentialism seeks a coherent system. London, poor and lacking the certitudes of a middle-class existence, spends his life working out from the materials of his life's experience his own brand of morality, which act is the very essence of existentialism. He is Man Alone, inventing an internal god as he goes.

He finds that god in the great symbol of the Northland.

The minority has always been "Man Alone," whether that minority be Eugene Donatlo's hero in *Christ in Concrete*, Henry Roth's hero in *Call It Sleep,* or the Invisible Man of Ralph Ellison. The difference between these citified heroes and Jack London's, however, is worth noting, for his heroes are not only alone culturally—a motley crew of white-trash outcasts and faceless Eskimos—but also alone in a land which is dead literally for a third part of the year. His Northland provides the perfect setting in which to examine the human soul's true nature, its primordial inclinations, its inherent conflicts. Frederick Feied notes, in his book *No Pie in the Sky*:

> The closing of the frontier gave perhaps the first indication that the pattern of the society of limited opportunity was beginning to repeat itself. With the consolidation of the Industrial Revolution in the nineteenth century and the rapid emergence of the industrial capitalist class as the dominant force in politics as well as economics, the ring was closed. It needed only

the panic of 1873, the first prolonged depression of the
new industrial era, to make the picture complete. With
its 2,000,000 to 3,000,000 unemployed, its bitterly
fought strikes, its promulgation of class ideologies, so
reminiscent of the period of the Hampden Clubs and
the machine wreckers in England, it set the stage for
the reappearance of the sturdy beggar in the person of
the dispossessed farmer and the unemployed migra-
tory worker.

It was this closed frontier that my family found, that we
Americans have grown up in, that is the nasty truth underlying what was once "The American Dream." Writing about
America generally and the West particularly, D. H. Lawrence,
another working-class writer, in his essay "Bottom Dogs,"
says:

> When we think of America, and of her huge success,
> we never realise how many failures have gone, and still
> go, to build up that success. It is not till you live in
> America, and go a little under the surface, that you be-
> gin to see how terrible and brutal is the mass of failure
> that nourishes the roots of the gigantic tree of dollars.
> And this is especially so in the country, and in the
> newer parts of the land, particularly out west. There
> you see how many small ranches have gone broke in
> despair, before the big ranches scoop them up and
> profit by all the back-breaking, profitless, grim labour
> of the pioneer. In the west you can still see the pioneer
> work of tough, hard first-comers, individuals, and it is
> astounding to see how often these individuals, pioneer
> first-comers who fought like devils against their dif-
> ficulties, have been defeated, broken, their efforts and
> their amazing hard work lost, as it were, in the face of
> the wilderness.

The West was once a land of opportunity, but it is now a closed frontier, and if a person is not born properly, that person might as well have been branded with the mark of Cain.

This closed frontier and its limitations has crippled what was once "American," the spirit of Emerson and Thoreau. I've tried living off the land—tried it when I was unemployed at the age of eighteen. I first tried sleeping in the fields of California's Central Valley, and got run off by farmers. I then went to Yosemite National Park and camped, but after two weeks was run off the park—there's a two-week camping limit. Tried the beach, the redwood forests, the deserts: every piece of land in America is now *property*, and therefore unavailable to a person who would try to merely live. Life outside of society is now impossible.

As it was becoming in London's time. He spent his time on the road as a hobo, and he wrote a book about it. The road is an escape valve for the downtrodden—if you can keep a step ahead of the law. The road might have been, in the days before London was born, a place like his Northland, a place where a person could discover himself. Nonetheless, the road provides an out for many an Oaklander. London writes in "The Tramp":

> If he have fought the hard fight, he is not unacquainted with the lure of the "road." When out of work and still undiscouraged, he has been forced to "hit the road" between large cities in his quest for a job. He has loafed, seen the country and green things, laughed in joy, lain on his back and listened to the birds singing overhead, unannoyed by factory whistles and bosses' harsh commands; and, most significant of all, *he has lived*. That is the point! He has not starved to death. Not only has he been care-free and happy, but he has lived! And from the knowledge that he has idled and is still alive, he achieves a new outlook on life; and the

more he experiences the unenviable lot of the poor
worker, the more the blandishments of the "road"
take hold of him. And finally he flings his challenge
in the face of society, imposes a valorous boycott on
all work, and joins the far-wanderers of Hoboland, the
gypsy folk of this latter day.

Life outside of society, though, since the closing of the frontier, doesn't work. London was eventually jailed and beaten in
New York. Life *inside* of society, on the other hand, if you're
at the bottom, is wretched. London writes,

The lower on the employment in the industrial scale,
the harder the conditions. The finer, the more delicate,
the more skilled the trade, the higher it is lifted above
the struggle. There is less pressure, less sordidness,
less savagery. There are fewer glass-blowers in proportionate to the needs of the glass-blowing industry than
there are ditch-diggers proportionate to the needs of
the ditch-digging industry. And not only this, for it
requires a glass-blower to take the place of a striking
glass-blower, while any kind of a striker or out-of-work
can take the place of a ditch-digger. So the skilled
trades are more independent, have more individuality
and latitude. The may confer with their masters, make
demands, assert themselves. The unskilled laborers,
on the other hand, have no voice in their affairs. The
settlement of terms is none of their business. "Free
contract" is all that remains to them. They may take
what is offered, or leave it. There are plenty more of
their kind. They do not count. They are members of
the surplus labor army, and must be content with a
hand-to-mouth existence.

Life at the bottom strips the humanity from man and makes
a thinking beast of him. This thinking beast is a creature that

suffers, but which does not contemplate. If the thinking beast is removed, though, and located outside of society amid nature, and, if the refined man a-roost at the top end of society is removed and located amid that same nature, the humanity that bubbles to the top is an essence, a distillate.

Of course, today this is impossible, for there is no tract of land for the poor to inhabit—all land is owned. The poor degenerate into creatures even more despicable than London's "work beasts," for they are as near to mindless as my dog, Dexter, clouded and hazed with commercial advertising (look at the current ghetto "fashion" of wearing clothes which advertise products—Nikes, Reboks, designer labels readable from a distance of fifty yards: companies don't have to pay ghetto-dwellers to wear sandwich-board ads—no, the ghetto-dwellers actually *pay the companies* to advertise *for them!*) and the pacifier of cheap beer and television and subsistence pay even for the lazy, the incompetent, and the stupid.

The American ghettos of today are relatively cushy joints, and the folks living in them make better yearly incomes off welfare than I made during my first fifteen years of teaching college. Ghettos are made miserable by the crimes and sloth of the inhabitants. Ghetto-dwellers generally have running water, electricity, television sets, and automobiles. They have the health care that not even adjunct college professors have. If they get sick, they go to the emergency room.

No one starves in the ghettos of America. Not from lack of resources they don't. Ghetto starvation is a matter of choice these days, folks choosing dope over food, choosing to feed consumer and drug habits before feeding themselves or their children.

In the ghettos of America you're more likely to find hideous distorted four-hundred-pound monsters of unrecognizable curd, their faces swollen with deep-fried slop and beers and Fritos, than you are to find even one hungry person. Richard O'Connor quotes London saying of America in 1916, "We stand for nothing except fat. We are become the fat man of the nations, whom nobody loves." Although London has sympathy for the ghetto, having grown up in it, he has a revulsion for the ghetto and its inhabitants that is unequivocal; the ghetto-dwellers in *The Iron Heel* are described thusly:

> I had seen the people of the abyss before, gone through its ghettos, and thought I knew it; but I found that I was now looking on it for the first time. . . . It surged past my vision in concrete waves of wrath, snarling and growling, carnivorous, drunk with whiskey from pillaged warehouses, drunk with hatred, drunk with lust for blood—men, women, and children, in rags and tatters, dim ferocious intelligences with all the god-like blotted from their features and all the fiend-like stamped in, apes and tigers, anaemic consumptives and great hairy beasts of burden, wan faces from which vampire society had sucked the juice of life, bloated forms swollen with physical grossness and corruption, withered hags and death's-heads bearded like patriarchs, festering youth and festering age, faces of fiends, crooked, twisted, misshapen monsters with the ravages of disease and all the horrors of chronic malnutrition—the refuse and the scum of life, a raging, screaming, screeching, demoniacal horde.

Imagine what he would have said had he borne witness to the ghettos of today, where ghetto-dwellers are funded through college, where ghetto-dwellers buy better food with food-stamps than working college students do after paying tuition, where the people of the ghetto wear $150 tennis shoes and are clad in the latest styles. The humorist P. J. O'Rourke says, "the biblical injunction is to clothe the naked, not style them," but the current culture of feel-goodness does not jibe with Mr. O'Rourke. Our ghetto-dwellers are sold the lie that they can become President some day, that they are special because they're human beings, that they are absolutely equal to millionaires and Harvard graduates. And they believe the lies!

As D. H. Lawrence writes in his essay "Americans," "We've got to pay for it, when you've made them feel that they're gods. A hundred million American godlets is rather much for the world to deal with."

Because our poor in America are no longer poor truly or even relatively in terms of worldwide standards, it's difficult for us to even imagine the sheer determination it must have taken a hundred years ago to rise out of the dungeon of humanity. Social programs in America have seen to it that we have the fattest poor people in the history of mankind.

Writing in *The People of the Abyss* of the children of the ghetto, London says that they

> possess all the qualities which make for noble manhood and womanhood; but the Ghetto itself, like an infuriated tigress turning on its young, turns upon and destroys all these qualities, blots out the light and laughter, and moulds those it does not kill into sodden and forlorn creatures, uncouth, degraded and wretched below the beasts of the field.

London is writing of a ghetto for which there is no social relief, and he sees in the people nobility that is crushed by environment. He believes that the ghetto-dwellers can be restored, if caught early enough, to dignity, although he concedes that this is a mighty trick indeed. He says, "In such conditions, the outlook for children is hopeless. They die like flies, and those that survive, survive because they possess excessive vitality and a capacity of adaptation to the degradation with which they are surrounded." But he adds, after cataloging the horrors to which these children are exposed, "The sort of men and women the survivors will make can readily be imagined."

Whereas in the impoverished ghettos of London's time, the very struggle for existence, for *subsistence* kept the people sharp, kept them plotting and scheming and using all available means *to survive*, today's ghetto-dwellers eat and sleep and breed and watch television, all their basic needs supplied by the state—housing secured, utilities functional, bellies swollen to the point of bursting. London envisions these folks off their asses and in the middle of a frozen wasteland, Arctic air freezing their fat solid, the environment altering the consciousness. Even the most seemingly stupid of human brutes, when confronted with the expanse of abyss and an environment that kills without human intervention, rises. London's fiction works toward a theory of the betterment of man through a program of self-exploration available through nature.

Much of London's fiction deals with the human garbage at the bottom of the social pit—hoboes, outcasts, bums, criminals. He even considers himself one of them. In a February 1911 letter to the "Comrades of the Mexican Revolution," he writes:

> We socialists, anarchists, hobos, chicken thieves, out-
> laws and undesirable citizens of the United States are
> with you heart and soul in your efforts to overthrow
> slavery and autocracy in Mexico. You will notice we
> are not respectable in these days of the reign of prop-
> erty. All the names you are being called, we have been
> called. And when graft and greed get up and begin
> to call names, honest men, brave men, patriotic men
> and martyrs can expect nothing else than to be called
> chicken thieves and outlaws.

So be it. But I for one wish that there were more chicken thieves and outlaws of the sort that formed the gallant band that took Mexicali, of the sort that is heroically enduring the prison holes of Diaz, of the sort that is fighting and dying and sacrificing in Mexico today.

I subscribe myself a chicken thief and a revolutionist,

Jack London

This could easily be considered the posturing of an armchair Socialist, but the problem is that London can't shake the ghetto from his bones. No matter how much success he might attain, he still sees himself as a poor boy. And he consistently writes of the scum at the bottom of society's barrel because he's afraid he might slip back down into that barrel. He wants to understand them so as to catch himself before he falls into their pit.

He's obsessed with "the submerged tenth."

Know thy enemy. Know thyself.

But he also writes of the bottom layer of humanity, because it's there he finds the primordial, the beast, that creature which is most truly human: man in his purest form, struggling for existence. The Naturalist obsession with ghettos and the poor is the obsession with uncovering the bare essentials of humanity, the human self outside of the safety net of society. In the ghettos of the late 19th- and early 20th-centuries in America were an amateur sociologist's dream. There one could find the human being reduced to his most animal state.

Our baser instincts flourished there.

Our most heroic qualities flourished there as well.

But the human garbage of the ghetto, even before social programs, was tainted. Ghettos were still subject to the unnatural whims of the market economy. The "trickle-down" theory of Republican economics sometimes actually worked, however minimally.

To find out what garbage we really are, and what warriors even garbage can be, you've got to get the garbage out of the city and onto the land.

London strands them in the White Silence.

In "The Tramp" London says about "the unfit, the inefficient, and mediocre" that

> at the bottom of the social pit, they are wretched, inarticulate beasts, living like beasts, breeding like beasts, dying like beasts. And how do they fare, these creatures born mediocre, whose heritage is neither brains nor brawn nor endurance? They are sweated in the slums in an atmosphere of discouragement and despair. There is no strength in weakness, no encouragement in foul air, vile food, and dank dens. They are there because they are so made that they are not fit to be higher up; but filth and obscenity do not strengthen the neck, nor does chronic emptiness of belly stiffen the back.

These folk make for good essays, and London's *The People of the Abyss* shows this. But they don't make for splendid fiction, at least not in London's mind. For in London's time there was an alternative to the ghetto: there was land in North America during London's time that had not yet become property. If a person didn't want to live in the squalor of the city or the poverty of a farm, that person could simply head for the frontier of the Northland.

No one today can *own* land outright. Not in this great nation they can't. Everyone must make money and pay their graft to the government. Land is taxed, and if you don't pay your taxes, you lose your home. There is not a single square inch of land a person can own in this our capitalist society. But in London's time, you could homestead still in Alaska.

You could walk into the forest, stake a claim, and say, "This plot of earth is mine." Which is why he went to the North.

"It was in the Klondike that I found myself," he writes. "There nobody talks. Everybody thinks. You get your perspective. I got mine."

The frozen wastes of the Northland—that's where philosophers should be forced to spend their doctoral years. It's where the welfare community should be located. It's where whining existentially bored sufferers of middle-class malaise and ennui should be spending their paid vacations.

Jack London uses the Northland as a testing ground for discovering the elemental common denominators of mankind, the heroic virtues as well as the vile and hideous traits we seem to universally share. It's easy to see London's reasoning. Alone, a vast black cosmos above and a barren frozen horizon broken by the white architecture of jagged cones of mountained ice, one's own breath the only sign of life, the White Silence throws the solitude of man back upon himself. The introspection of our age—the disgusting narcissism of talk shows; the confessional fiction of slick magazines; and the lowest form of literature of our day, the "personal essay" —is the stuff of spoiled babies whining about middle-class insecurities, writers howling for their mama's nipples because they're wondering whether or not there's a reason for their sadness, their unidentifiable pain. Toss them into the Klondike for a winter, and their songs would change.

The working poor don't see shrinks.

They're too busy working.

It's only when man has too much leisure that he collapses upon himself and dares the Kurtzian horror of self-evaluation.

Unless that horror is forced upon man.

In his fiction, London works out a way to force that horror upon his characters.

And upon us.

V

The City's Sons

It is a mistake to believe that the people don't read London's lesser works, or to claim, as Richard O'Connor does in his 1964 biography, that

> [t]he city fathers [of Oakland] . . . have long since forgiven him not only his political views but the reputation he earned as a saloon brawler, a libertine and a notably free spirit . . . not to mention a record for juvenile delinquency that has seldom (if we take his own word for it) been surpassed.

What O'Connor does not recognize, or perhaps what wasn't evident when he wrote his biography, is that the "city fathers" are the city's sons. Oakland's mayors for the past thirty years have been black, and the only newspaper left in town, *The Oakland Tribune*, reads like a modern version of *New Masses*: Democratic, if not Socialist in bent. It's not that the city fathers have forgiven London's views; it's that they all too well understand, if not embrace them. Just as London railed about the supremacy of the white race when Oakland was populated with poor whites, now blacks make the same claim. The substitution has been easier than one would think. Philip S. Foner, in his essay "American Rebel," cites Martin Russak writing for a 1929 issue of *New Masses*:

Workers who read, read Jack London. He is the one author they have all read, he is one literary experience they all have in common. Factory workers, farm hands, seamen, miners, newsboys read him and read him again. He is the most popular writer of the American working class.

In *The Western Canon* Harold Bloom writes, "Very few working-class readers ever matter in determining the survival of texts." He's about as far off as a critic can get on this one. If he were right, Jack London's works would have gone out of print long ago.

In Oakland, our diet of London begins in grammar school and continues throughout high school. Oakland's children, by the time they graduate from high school, know what a Socialist is, and they know that London felt contempt for "the mob-minded mass." Poor and working-class Oakland children, black, white, Mexican or Chinese, however, feel in their hearts that they are budding Jack Londons: this is what we are taught in school by English teachers who themselves once considered themselves to be budding Jack Londons. London's experience is ours, and his success can be ours too, we're taught. London, writing in a letter about his youth, says,

Fred worked in the cannery for a short summer vacation—aye the reward was to be a term at college. I worked in the same cannery, not for a vacation but for a year. For months at a time, during that year, I was up and at work at six in the morning. I took half an hour for dinner. I took half an hour for supper. I worked every night till ten, eleven and twelve o'clock. My wages were small, but I worked such long hours that I sometimes made as high as fifty dollars a month. Duty—I turned every cent over. Duty—I have worked in that hell hole for thirty-six straight hours, at a machine, and I was only a child. I remember how I was trying to save the money to buy a skiff—eight dollars. All that summer I saved and scraped. In the fall I had five dollars as a result of absolutely doing without all pleasure. My mother came to the machine where I worked and asked for it. I could have killed myself that night. After a year of hell to have that pitiful—to be robbed of that petty joy.

This story is the story of most of the people I grew up with. We didn't get "allowances"—we worked and forked over the cash to our parents. While the rich kids in the distant Oakland Hills and in the suburbs were getting cars from their parents, we were buying the family groceries. When we got thrown out of our trailer for unsanitary living conditions, my brothers and I had to sell all our possessions—our bicycles, our athletic shoes, our football and our baseball bat, our coin collections, our 8-track tapes—to help our father raise the cash for the security deposit on an apartment in the ghetto. London's story is *our* story.

In *Jack London: An American Myth*, John Perry would have us believe that London was joshing us when he told of his days as a worker. Concerning London's shipping out as a seaman, Perry writes, "Did Jack London stretch his feats of the *Sophie Sutherland*? Written years later, perhaps he confused fact with fancy—or did he ever go to sea? That remains the biggest mystery," and as evidence of his doubts, Perry poses a series of questions: "Why would a captain accept London? He had slight knowhow, sensitive hands and feet, couldn't swim well, and was poorly coordinated. Could such a teenager survive schooner life?" Reading this makes my blood boil, and if I ever get the chance to meet Mr. Perry, I'll give the sheltered ninny an earful.

Q. Why would a captain accept London?

A. London was breathing and willing to work.

Q. What about those sensitive hands, those sensitive feet?

A. Let's watch them bleed!

Q. He can't swim.

A. Let him drown.

Q. Could such a teenager survive schooner life?

A. If he can't, we'll get another. There are many more where this one comes from.

Mr. Perry doesn't know a damned thing about how blue-collar jobs are won. He's one of those people who thinks everything he reads in the newspapers is true, who gets his hands on a union contract or a law and believes that because something is in print, the world operates that way. He'd have us believe that the "rules" are followed, and society operates in an orderly, structured fashion. People like Perry come to construction sites wearing suits and scan the working beasts and see the exhausted men taking a break from their jackhammers and shovels and assume that they're shirking their duties.

When I was a construction worker and between jobs, I'd get up at four in the morning, put on my tool belt and a hardhat, and go to a construction site, showing up before the other workers. And I'd wait, stand around the site like a vulture. I'd wait for someone to miss work from being hungover, I'd wait for someone to lose a limb, I'd wait for someone to be crushed to death by a falling girder, I'd wait for someone to get an eye burned out by an errant torch flame. It never took me more than a week to get a job. Someone would get an arm chopped off, and the foreman would give me the nod before the severed limb was even put into an ice chest. I'd be working before the foreman knew my name. That's how things work in the real blue-collar world. That's how they work in Oakland, in *my* Oakland. In *Jack London's* Oakland.

Oakland is Jack London's town, and Jack London is its favorite son. Although Oakland features a small population of fairly well-off middle-class folks, most people who live in Oakland live in squalor.

Beware if an Oaklander gets an education, though. Jack London did, and "His reading did not make him long for the best of thought, rather for the worst: —Revolution, destruction, dissipation, and passionate indulgence"—that according to his schoolmate and friend Georgia Loring Bamford. Education of the poor is a dangerous thing indeed, because when the poor figure out how they're getting screwed, they go blind with fury. The youth of Oakland tend to be young Socialists who, if they achieve worldly success, find themselves in a paradoxical situation: Socialist in sympathies while at the same time scorning those whom they perceive to have neither the will nor capacity for upward mobility.

For my high school graduation present, my father gave me a sleeping bag and a Coleman ice chest. I didn't need to have the gift explained: I started the engine of my '67 Dodge Polara and I drove. I'd saved two hundred dollars from scrubbing smoke from the furniture of burned-out houses, and I drove for two days along the back roads of California's Central Valley, alongside the sloughs and levees that kept the valley from flooding each Spring. Sometimes I'd stop in a farm town, Lodi or Merced or Oakdale, Crow's Landing or Red Bluff, Redding, and when I stopped I'd walk into the office of a company and lie my way into a job. "Damn straight I can weld! What the hell you think I been doing to keep myself alive these past three years if I ain't been welding?" And I'd get the job. It usually took at least a few days before they figured out I didn't know shit from Shinola, and they'd fire my ass and send me packing. But I'd have a check in pocket, and some work experience, and in this fashion I worked my way up and down the West Coast, learning how to lie, learning how to work. I ended up in Alaska.

California may seem to have no culture, to be a void no anthropologist would bother to study, no archaeologist would bother to unearth. But Californians have culture indeed, and our culture is Work. Unlike the East, which has always been no more than an extension of England in its early days and greater Europe as time progressed, and unlike the South which was founded on the Spaniard/English colonial itch, and unlike the farmland wasteland between the Appalachians and the Rockies, the West, and more specifically, California, is a land forged outside of everything European and Mid-western and Southern: California is a land whose museums are afterthoughts, superimposed cultural icons sprinkled over the state when Easterners invaded for their share of the banking industry after gold was discovered in '48. And this is why Steinbeck and London are our two great writers: they don't write, like Harold Brodkey, about some ninny New Yorker who cut his thumb and got sad when his wife didn't sympathize. They don't do the sappy Updike dance of suburban sentimentality. No, they write about people at work, together with other people working, alone in the cosmos of their physical and spiritual labors.

California is a land of criminals who fled the East and had to stop when they reached the edge of the continent. Every disgruntled sociopath, every person who got run out of town after town, ended up in California. The worst of them ended up in Oakland.

Jack London was their progeny.

And so am I.

So you won't find a California writer writing about parlor room intrigue, because in California most of us have never even seen a parlor room, and those of us who have don't end up writers. You won't find a California writer's characters wandering through museums and strolling their dogs through parks. No golden bowl would ever be the critical element of a California novel—more likely it would be an iron girder, a rusted shovel, a tire-iron, a backhoe, a jackhammer, a broken bottle of Thunderbird or Night Train, a roll of tie-wire. More likely the critical element of a California novel would be a stain on the waitress's apron, a scar on the longshoreman's chest, a human skull hidden in the basement.

In California, people respect picket lines. California is a land of work, and the Socialist element is alive and strong. London writes, in an article printed in the *Atlantic Monthly*:

> After God had finished the rattlesnake, the toad and the vampire, he had some awful substance left with which He made a SCAB. A SCAB is a two-legged animal with a corkscrew soul, a water-logged brain, and a combination backbone made of jelly and glue. Where others have hearts he carries a tumor of rotten principles.
>
> When a SCAB comes down the street men turn their backs and angels weep in heaven, and the devil shuts the gates of hell to keep him out. No man has a right to SCAB as long as there is a pool of water deep enough to drown his body in, or a rope long enough to hang his carcass with. Judas Iscariot was a gentleman compared with a SCAB. For betraying his Master, he had character enough to hang himself. A SCAB HASN'T!

Scabs are indeed despised creatures in California. The union strikes at the turn of the century in San Francisco are famous, and the spirit lives on. Even the union-busting Reagan and Bush years haven't destroyed the spirit of the unions in the state.

My union card is a matter or pride for me. I wouldn't give it up for the world. Once I'm tenured, I'll spend the rest of my days unionizing the scabs of academia: the adjunct slave army. In California, I'd be able to do it. Scabs are detested, and when they are found dead in parking lots, people generally think they had it coming. As London writes in "The Scab":

> When a striker kills with a brick the man who has taken his place, he has no sense of wrong-doing. In the deepest holds of his being, though he does not reason the impulse, he has an ethical sanction. He feels dimly that he has justification, just as the home-defending Boer felt, though more sharply, with each bullet he fired at the invading English. Behind every brick thrown by a striker is the selfish will "to live" of himself, and the slightly altruistic will "to live" of his family. The family group came into the world before the State group, and society, being still on the primitive basis of tooth and nail, the will "to live" of the State is not so compelling to the striker as is the will "to live" of his family and himself.

The "primordial" that London is often belittled for being obsessed with is the norm for vast numbers of Californians—it is, after all, the largest manufacturing state in the union. The workers feel their closeness to the beast of man, and with each dollar that is wrung from them they grow more animal. They bite against anything that would rob them of their daily bread. Elsewhere in "The Scab," London writes that, in a competitive society,

> [w]ise old saws to the contrary, he who takes from a man's purse takes from his existence. To strike at a man's food and shelter is to strike at his life; and in a society organized on a tooth-and-nail basis, such an act, performed though it may be under the guise of generosity, is none the less menacing and terrible.

It is for this reason that a laborer is so fiercely hostile to another laborer who offers to work for less pay or longer hours. To hold his place, (which is to live), he must offset this offer by another equally liberal, which is equivalent to giving away somewhat from the food and shelter he enjoys. To sell his day's work for $2 instead of $2.50, means that he, his wife, and his children will not have so good a roof over their heads, so warm clothes on their backs, so substantial food in their stomachs. Meat will be bought less frequently and it will be tougher and less nutritious, stout new shoes will go less often on the children's feet, and disease and death will be more immanent in a cheaper house and neighborhood.

Thus the generous laborer, giving more of a day's work for less return, (measured in terms of food and shelter), threatens the life of his less generous brother laborer, and at the best, if he does not destroy that life, he diminishes it. Whereupon the less generous laborer looks upon him as an enemy, and, as men are inclined to do in a tooth-and-nail society, he tries to kill the man who is trying to kill him.

When workers figure out how Capitalism works, they grow more likely to be Socialist. As well, they grow more violent concerning their possessions, for workers can look around their living quarters and tell you exactly how much each commodity cost. They can tell you the prices of the food at the grocery store, the prices of new socks and the price of a telephone call. And when they're calculating the prices, they're calculating the prices in term of hours worked at horrid jobs. If someone steals a worker's television set, and the set cost $400, and the worker makes $200 per week, then not only has the thief stolen a $400 television set, but, in the worker's mind, the thief has *stolen two weeks of life*. For work is not life. It's death. It's what one does when one is not alive. James L. Blewer writes, "Your average factory worker is more of a Marxist than Terry Eagleton ever will be," and the factory worker will be a Marxist without even knowing it.

London, however, turned against Socialism increasingly as he made more cash, as he got further away from his ghetto sumptank roots. The more cash he made, the more parlor rooms he gained entrance into, the more he despised those who were once his comrades. He saw workers as morons or lazy asses, and repeatedly drove the point home that he would have nothing to do with the "work beasts" treading toxic water in the toilet bowl of industrial humanity.

Jack London's eventual scorn for Socialism is aptly articulated in a letter dictated to his wife Charmian and published in the *Socialist Press*, dated 7 March 1916:

> My final word is that Liberty, freedom, and independence are royal things that cannot be presented to, nor thrust upon, races or classes. If races and classes cannot rise up and by their strength of brain and brawn, wrest from the world liberty, freedom, and independence, they never in time can come to these royal possessions—and if such royal things are kindly presented to them by superior individuals, on silver platters, they will know not what to do with them, will fail to make use of them, and will be what they have always been in the past . . . inferior races and inferior classes.

Charmian London, after he dictated the letter, asked him, "And now . . . what will you call yourself henceforth—Revolutionist, Socialist, what?" to which he replied, "I am not anything, I fear. . . . I am all these things. Individuals disappoint me more and more, and more and more I turn to the land."

In *No Pie in the Sky: The Hobo as American Cultural Hero in the Works of Jack London, John Dos Passos, and Jack Kerouac*, Frederick Feied writes:

> Darwin and Nietzsche on the one hand; Marx and Engels on the other; London was to feel the attraction of these opposites all his life, and all his life he continued to play with their fascinating parallels—parallels that moved like warring armies to diametrically opposed conclusions.

Like most critics, Feied makes no attempt to reconcile London's apparent contradictions. London, quite simply (in the mind of the critics), was confused or, perhaps, merely a hypocrite.

But London is indeed working out these seeming contradictions in his work, and what might seem contradictory at first makes sure sense when you consider the horrid town of Oakland. The problem most critics have understanding London's seeming contradictions is this: most professors have never feared that they would starve. Most professors have never *actually been homeless*. Most professors have never been beaten on a work site that they were not free to leave. Most professors have only a theoretical understanding of poverty, of labor, of the absolute horror and fright of what it is to grow up in a place where your life is in danger every second, and if, by some miracle, you don't get killed or beaten by the ghetto pigs, then you hear your belly rumbling like an earthquake.

I was in the Laborers Union, Local 304, Oakland, for twelve years, seven of which I was active as a concrete worker, a guniter, a lumper, a ditch-digger, a rip-rapper, an asphalt worker, a demolitionist, and a worker at variety of other jobs. I saw seven men die on the jobsite. One I saw worked to death in the 110-degree heat of Bishop, California, just northwest of Death Valley. We were working twelve-hour days, seven days a week, with no breaks for food, for using the bathroom, for getting a drink of water. If we stopped working, we were fired. If we stopped working and we were Mexican, and illegal, we were deported. And that's how Little Joe died. He was overweight and he kept passing out, and when he'd pass out, the foreman would kick him or slap him or dump a bucket of concrete-gray water on him, and the foreman would say, "If you don't want to get sent back to Mexico, get your ass back up and go to work, you fat fuck." And Little Joe would get back up, stagger to the concrete we were working (we were making a sewage holding tank the size of three football fields), and get back to his labor. Then one time he dropped, his body convulsed, he fouled his pants, and he was dead. The foreman dragged him up the slope by tying him with a rope and dragging him behind his pickup truck. Little Joe's body was ripped by the re-bar and iron spikes on the slope, chunks of meat and blood dangling and oozing from the metal. The foreman called the union hall on the radio and had another worker out there on the job site in fifteen minutes.

I saw two men lose their legs when I was working in an open sewer; the black tar sewer sludge got into their waders and poisoned the men. Their legs had to be amputated that day.

I saw a man die because he was forced (again at the threat of being deported) to climb scaffolding that was not secured to the building. The scaffolding fell over, and the man splattered on the street like a pumpkin. The foreman had first ordered me to climb that scaffolding, and I'd told him no. He fired me. When the Mexican died, the foreman rushed to my car and rehired me. He was a man short.

Any man who has seen these kinds of horrors, these kinds of abuse made possible by capitalism and the threat of losing one's job and therefore one's life, naturally has a sympathy for the working class, for the work beasts at the bottom of society, in the Pit. Seeing these kinds of things makes a man wish death on the oppressors, on the capitalists, on the rich and the bourgeoisie. Watch a man get worked to death, and know it could have been you lying there on the ground, and *if you know in your heart it could have been you*, tell me that you don't believe the workers deserve a better shake.

Now imagine: you have escaped. You are no longer a work beast. You control your own destiny, and you did it through brainpower. This is what happens: you look back on the brutes in the cellar of society, and although you have compassion for them, although you all too well know what they're going through, you reach this conclusion: if they would have worked as hard as you, if they had had your smarts, if they, like you, were *superior* human beings, they would not have found themselves forever in the Pit. If you've escaped the true Pit, the hell which is beneath working-class America, you can't help but think that anyone who hasn't escaped is not as good as you are. Why should you do anything for them, after all, when you made it out on your own?

In London's oft-reprinted essay, "How I Became a Socialist," collected in *War of the Classes*, he describes the onset of this double set of sympathies:

> It is quite fair to say that I became a Socialist in a fashion somewhat similar to the way in which the Teutonic pagans became Christians—it was hammered into me. Not only was I not looking for Socialism at the time of my conversion, but I was fighting it. I was very young and callow, did not know much of anything, and though I had never even heard of a school called "Individualism," I sang the paean of the strong with all my heart.

This was because I was strong myself. By strong I mean that I had good health and hard muscles, both of which possessions are easily accounted for. I had lived my childhood on California ranches, my boyhood hustling newspapers on the streets of a healthy Western city, and my youth on the ozone-laden waters of San Francisco Bay and the Pacific Ocean. I loved life in the open, and I toiled in the open, at the hardest kinds of work. Learning no trade, but drifting along from job to job, I looked on the world and called it good, every bit of it. Let me repeat, this optimism was because I was healthy and strong, bothered with neither aches nor weaknesses, never turned down by the boss because I did not look fit, able always to get a job at shovelling coal, sailorizing, or manual labor of some sort.

London, then, was a fairly successful young grunt, working away and basking in his laborial youth. The weak? He writes, "As for the unfortunates, the sick, and ailing, and old, and maimed, I must confess I hardly thought of them at all, save that I vaguely felt that they, barring accidents, could be as good as I if they wanted to real hard, and could work just as well." When you have your strength, your youth, and the ability to quit one nasty job and take on another nasty job without missing a day's work, it's difficult to have sympathy for anyone else, especially the failures. Failures are simply those who don't measure up. They are those one has defeated in the animal kingdom of life. But London himself got kicked around eventually. He went across the country, ended up in jail in upstate New York, where he was beaten and abused, and, he says,

> I found myself looking upon life from a new and totally different angle. I had dropped down from the

proletariat into what sociologists love to call "the submerged tenth," and I was startled to discover the way
in which that submerged tenth was recruited. I found
there all sorts of men, many of whom had once been
as good as myself and just as blond beastly; sailor-men,
soldier-men, labor-men, all wrenched and distorted
and twisted out of shape by toil and hardship and accident, and cast adrift by their masters like so many
old horses.

Cast adrift like Little Joe, like the Mexicans I saw get their legs
eaten off by sewer poisoning, cast adrift like any worker who
can't cut the mustard in America. In a capitalist society, unless
I am making the loot, I am as useless as a rodent. When I hear
of rich people (people who own homes, who have health care,
who have full-time jobs) losing their homes, their families,
their lives to fire and flood and earthquake and disease, I am
happy. I should feel some sense of shame about this, but I
don't. They don't feel any sense of shame about me when I'm
teaching their children in college classrooms for a pittance
and haven't been able to afford a visit to a dentist in four
years. *They, they, they*—those good folk who by their very
existence rob me of my dignity. The Social Pit, as London
calls it, is a very real thing to me, and London writes, along
the same lines in "How I Became a Socialist":

> I saw the picture of the Social Pit as vividly as though
> it were a concrete thing, and at the bottom of the Pit I
> saw them, myself above them, not far, and hanging on
> to the slippery wall by main strength and sweat. What
> when my strength failed? When I should be unable to
> work shoulder to shoulder with the strong men who
> were as yet babes unborn? And there and then I swore
> a great oath. It ran something like this: All my days I
> have worked hard with my body, and according to the

> number of days I have worked, by just that much am
> I nearer the bottom of the Pit. I shall climb out of the
> Pit, but not by the muscles of my body shall I climb
> out. I shall do no more hard work, and may God strike
> me dead if I do another day's hard work with my body
> more than I absolutely have to do. And I have been
> busy ever since running away from hard work.

Jack London's contradictions are not necessarily contradictions: they are the natural by-products of a man who has
escaped the ghetto. Listen to the rap lyrics of the now famous
Oakland bands: in one song, they're rapping to "fight the
power," to "kill the Man," and so forth—so many Socialist
slogans delivered in Ebonics; in the next song, they're singing
about how they likes they hot bitches and good drugs. By-
products, not contradictions.

Leonard Cassuto and Jeanne Campbell Reesman, in the
introduction to their recent selection of criticism, *Rereading
Jack London*, see London's work as a tangled mess:

> Though London saw value and challenge in Nietzsche's
> ideas (first available, it should be noted, in inaccurate
> translations), we suggest that his unsystematic, often
> self-contradictory worldview, buttressed by his ec-
> centric vision of "individualistic socialism," may be
> better described by Emersonian representativeness
> than by Nietzschean greatness and its accompanying
> discontents. (Indeed, London lamented what he saw
> as a critical misunderstanding of *The Sea Wolf* accord-
> ing to which he himself endorsed Nietzschean ideas.)
> The point here is not to trace literary influence—there
> is no evidence that Emerson made any significant
> impression on London. Instead, Emerson's metaphor
> is a helpful navigational tool to get through London's
> tangled ideas and—as will become clear—a way of

emphasizing the importance of London to American literary studies.

Their goal, like many others, is to attempt to superimpose a system of thought over London's work because they see Socialism and Individualism, "individualistic socialism," as being incompatible. Cassuto and Reesman resort to Emerson as a convenience, as Emerson's works are so all-encompassing that one can derive just about whatever social stance one wishes from them. But socialism and individualism are not mutually exclusive categories. It is possible to wish for socialism and still be a raging capitalist. Nay, it is necessary in a society in which socialism will most likely never be a reality. For howl all we would about the need for socialism, if the society we would have be socialist is *not* socialist, then we are fools to wallow in the Pit. And if we escape the Pit, we look at the people still in it with both compassion and contempt. This is London's contradiction. This is London's concern. He works to present these two mutually dependent, coexistent, and enduring sides of the American Dream's trick coin. The presentation of these two battling social philosophies, rather than weakening the power of London's work, instead actually enhances his work's appeal, for like it or not, in America we are all a bit Socialist, a bit Fascist. It's the by-product of democracy.

This is certainly the case with folks who've escaped the blue-collar hell of Oakland. Although there are many working-class cities which resemble Oakland, cities of workers within view of shining towers of commerce, cities such as Newark is to Manhattan, Spokane is to Seattle, Fort Worth is to Dallas, none is in the same historical and geographical situation as Oakland. Rising alongside San Francisco in the days of the Gold Rush, Oakland has always been a city ashamed of itself for its poverty and low status on the socioeconomic scale. At the same time, however, Oakland is proud, in a swaggering and swarthy blue-collar kind of way, of its machismo, its brutality, its Wild West individuality. Jack London is its primary spokesman. In *The Call of the Wild*, London transcends his ideology in the only way feasible, given the town he allowed to forge him. The book stands as a testimony to his life-long struggle to reconcile his beliefs with his success.

Even Oaklanders would like to think of themselves as nice folk, but the fact of the matter is this: in a capitalistic society, we succeed by stomping on the hopes, if not the very lives, of other people. My bread is at the expense of folks I've beat in the game of capitalism.

So was London's.

So is yours.

VI

Jack London and the Canon

First, this: I worship the canon.

As a writer and a scholar, I defend it with all my soul. I rave to my students and colleagues, I howl in book reviews, I harangue those who would substitute politically trendy authors for canonized authors as would a street preacher a passing prostitute. When I get rolling in defense of the canon, my heart rate increases, my speech quickens, and I need only a pulpit to make the picture complete.

Give me a crowd of New Historicists and a three-hour lecture, and I'll guarantee converts by the end of the lecture.

The canon has been my comfort, my instructor, my religion for nearly thirty years now. But the canon is not perfect. Not by a long shot.

Before becoming an ideological literary whipping boy, London was largely excluded from the academic canon. Harold Bloom doesn't even include London in his exhaustive reading list at the end of *The Western Canon*, while including the likes of poet Edward Hirsch, six books by Philip Roth, books by Richard Howard, James Applewhite, and Allen Grossman. The canon, however, is not formed by academics. And we're damned lucky it's not. For if it were, we'd find Alice Walker and Frederick Douglass occupying positions more important than Homer and Shakespeare.

I took the Code 64 GRE Subject Test in Literature a decade ago. On my exam, there were no questions that dealt with Milton. No questions on Pope, on Chaucer. Wordsworth wasn't on my test. There were only four questions on Shakespeare. There were eight questions on Chinua Achebe. Virgil and Homer and Dante weren't on the exam. Toni Morrison, Alice Walker, and James Baldwin were.

Bluntly: White males were sacrificed at the literary altar. To make room? To make amends? To punish the students who'd foolishly spent their time studying Milton, Chaucer, and Wordsworth? It's a sad day when the academic culture places Alice Walker above Homer. There's something rotten in the state of New Jersey. The academic culture, fortunately, does not create writers.

Critics who still maintain that the history of Western literature is sequential and interdependent and subject to the rigors of aesthetic judgment—critics who are now called, with an air of disdain, "conservative," as if they're the most wicked of Republicans—universally rue the present state of the canon as it is being handled by the generation of scholars reared on Derrida, Foucault, Barthes, Hartman, Lacan, and Jameson. And with good reason. This generation of scholars has taken it upon itself to pass on a fantastic theory to their students: that the history of influence and the interconnections between writers and generations and eras and epochs don't *actually* exist, that they are merely social constructs *of our times* and there to be dismantled. Criticism, not creative work, is what is important, and sitcom will do as well for a dissertation topic as Milton—nay, better, for the *Beverly Hillbillies* or *All in the Family* help to dismantle that "conservative" notion of value.

The text is secondary, the theory is primary, and the Author is Dead. When this silliness has passed, we'll return to the texts and their writers. For even Harold Bloom, one of the better-known critics of our times and a critic who seems often to change his mind about things, nearing the end of his career concedes, indeed *argues* that critics are not the dictators of the canon. He writes in *The Western Canon*:

> The deepest truth about secular canon-formation is that it is performed by neither critics nor academies, let alone politicians. Writers, artists, composers themselves determine canons, by bridging strong precursors and strong successors.

However, this is being undermined in our academies. In the classrooms of most of the dozen universities and colleges I've worked for, what's important is *making the students feel good about themselves*. One way to do this is by inflating the importance of texts that reflect each of their respective immediate experiences. Hence, in *The Heath Anthology of American Literature*, Mary Chestnut is ranked as being as canonical as Emerson and Thoreau, and the third-hand transcript of a speech made by Chief Seattle is equated with the work of Melville. Writers operating in cultural isolation, never having engaged the Western Canon on any level, are claimed to be entrenched in that canon by virtue of their *not having engaged* the canon. In other words, because the writers are outside of canonical experience, they are by definition part of the canon, the canon being redefined as that set of works that most represents the variety of cultural experience in America. A barely literate slave scribbling memoirs in an attic is equated with Emerson on the basis of *being different* from Emerson.

For better or worse, I don't know of a writer whose work is primarily influenced by Chief Seattle's speeches. I doubt Joyce had them in mind when he was cataloging Western literature in *Ulysses*. I doubt Flannery O'Connor or Katherine Anne Porter were studying the linguistic tropes, the narrative structure, the splendid style of Chief Seattle.

The notion of aesthetic quality of a text is under fire in today's academic culture. For the time being, didacticism is more important than aesthetics—given that the lesson being taught is the correct one.

I was once reprimanded by the Dean of a community college for which I was laboring. I was teaching a creative writing course, and after class one day a student who'd not yet presented work stopped me and handed me a folder.

"Read these," she said. "I wants to know what you thinks."

"I'll take them home," I said.

"I can't let you have them," she said. "They original."

So I opened the folder. It contained about fifty hand-written poems, dating back to when the student was most likely in elementary school. They were rhyming little ditties, very sincere, reminiscent of Dr. Seuss in a sad mood. I wrote the student a list of poets whose works I thought she might find useful, canonical poets from whose example the student might learn, might enrich her understanding of the possibilities of poetry which resembled her own—Beaudelaire, Keats, Dickinson, Langston Hughes, Michael S. Harper, Sylvia Plath. "You might read these poets," I said, "and then after reading these poets, revise your own poems."

She snatched her folder from me and began to scream at me, "These poems be from the heart." A security guard turned to watch what was happening. "These poems be from the heart. The heart don't need no revising!"

"Then don't show them to me," I said.

The next day, I came as close to being fired as I've ever come—for being racist against her and her self-expression. The threat of a lawsuit loomed unless I made a public and a personal written apology to the student for my racial insensitivity.

The canon in academia is synonymous with racism and sexism.

James L. Blewer writes,

> literature departments are full of people who walk
> around with their long antennae out searching for ways
> in which their own personal values (sexual, political,
> religious) have been offended. I once told a colleague
> of mine that I was doing some work on Flannery
> O'Connor, and her reply was, "Oh, she was a racist,
> wasn't she?" That's all she needed to know. . . . Henry
> James? A repressed homosexual who presumed to be
> able to write about women. John Milton? Those poor
> daughters he awakened in the middle of the night.
> James Joyce? Something of an anti-Semite, wasn't he?

Students have become *consumers*, and what they consume increasingly becomes what *they* want to consume, not what the
academy dictates as meet and proper for consumption. Education is becoming a product for purchase. The academic's
job becomes increasingly to give the students what they want,
not necessarily the truth.

But writers really don't give much a hoot what the academics think. Make the students read a token one-armed
deaf-mute crippled Polynesian leper, so that one-armed deaf
-mute crippled Polynesian lepers are represented, and it's still
not going to make the next generation of students follow the
one-armed deaf-mute crippled Polynesian leper's example—
not unless the leper is a truly great writer. And there is such
a thing as relative value in literature. We don't like to admit
it these twisted democratic sensitive days, but some folks are
better at things than other folks. Some people are smarter;
some are stronger; some are, in short, superior. We seem at
home with the idea only in sports, where no one would argue
that a pygmy is a better basketball player than Michael Jordan.
Try to argue that someone is more intelligent or more talented

than someone else, though, and you're looking to get sued, at least in academic circles.

Once a student threatened to sue me because my course syllabus for American Lit didn't include enough women. She didn't say which women she wanted included. There just weren't *enough women.*

Imagine if accounting professors were under fire to balance their syllabi with female accounting theorists, 19th-century African-American accounting theorists, 18th-century Native American accounting theorists.

Bloom writes in *The Western Canon*, "We are destroying all intellectual and aesthetic standards in the humanities and social sciences, in the name of social justice. Our institutions show bad faith in this: no quota are imposed upon brain surgeons or mathematicians."

London (who obviously influenced writers of the generation immediately following his own—writers such as Hemingway, Steinbeck, and Dos Passos—continues to be a strong literary force of influence in the writers of today, notably the writer whom I consider to be America's finest living author (and I'm not alone in this opinion), Cormac McCarthy. Fully one fourth of McCarthy's novel *The Crossing*, is told from the point of view of a wolf, and McCarthy's masterpiece, *Blood Meridian*, features as its main character a manifestation of Nietzsche's Übermensch in the form of Judge Holden, a land-lubbing version of Wolf Larsen of London's *The Sea Wolf*. London's influence on Norman Mailer is even more profound and full. Norman Mailer is today's Jack London, and seems to have modeled his literature and his life after London. Mailer is arguably our most famous literary personality, and more than happy, like London, to promote that fame. His books are uneven in quality, some disasters, a few works of genius. And the books cover a lot of ground, from ancient Egypt to World War II to the CIA. Mailer is a man's man, legendary for his proclivity for fisticuffs and violence, known for drunken brawls and vitriolic statements. He's as much a character as a writer, using himself by name in his novels at times, thinly veiling himself in other novels. There is a mythology of Mailer accompanied by Mailer spottings and rumors and anecdotes. Like London, he ran for mayor of his home city and bombed. If there has ever been a writer who molded himself in London's image, it has been Norman Mailer. A writer who is a member of the canon, though, is not merely a writer who influences other writers, but also a writer who has been *influenced by* the writers in the canon. A canonical writer comes from and leads to great literature.

The literary canon is this: those works to which subsequent authors turn for guidance. The canon is the group of works authors, not literary critics, read. For today there might be an academic conference on the forgotten writer Bunion B. Corn, and the academics might publish their papers and their books, but be sure of this: if the writers themselves don't turn to Bunion B. Corn, Bunion B. Corn will not enter the canon. He will be forgotten when the wave of scholars who took interest in Corn dies off or retires. Understood thusly, no matter how many times a student has Frederick Douglass shoved down his throat, Douglass won't become part of the canon unless those students become writers and *then* turn to Douglass for instruction and inspiration. Jane Smiley, try as she might in the periodicals to prove that Mark Twain stinks, fails as long as writers keep on reading *Hucklberry Finn*. Hemingway is commonly and conspicuously omitted from anthologies—some kind of political statement, I suspect—but writers continue to read Papa's books. Henry Miller might not make doctoral exam lists, and he might not be taught in a seminar at a university, but the writers themselves—Norman Mailer,

Jack Kerouac, Lawrence Ferlinghetti, Karl Shapiro, Donald Barthelme, and a host of other prominent figures—have turned to him. Though not canonized by the university, he is canonized by the writers, the true makers of the canon.

And so Jack London: search as we might through the anthologies, we don't find him in most of the standard textbooks. America's most famous writer around the world, now over a century dead, doesn't make the cut above such hacks as Denise Chavez; Amy Tan; the brilliantly boring John Barth; the politically powerful (in American letters, at least) yet ultimately shallow John Updike; the vacuous (and proud of it!) Bobbie Ann Mason; the rapidly fading, now that he's as dead as the suburbs about which he wrote, John Cheever; but, although he's not anthologized, London remains, and not merely as a topic of critical vitriol or biographical curiosity or sensationalism. London remains because writers read him, because children read him, because workers read him, because the world over his works are read by every class of people who can read at all and who wish to read the work of an American. He remains because his influence is *pervasive.* Even those who haven't read Jack London since they were children, even people who have never read Jack London at all, have a sense of who he is. Like Shakespeare and Dickens and Hemingway and Dickinson and Wordsworth, London is a state, a condition, a cultural force even the illiterate and ill-read are familiar with. People who haven't read Shakespeare still have a feeling of what Shakespeare is, of what Shakespeare means. Likewise with Jack London.

If writers and nonwriters, if Americans and foreigners, if academics and the little-learned read Jack London, then certainly there must be more to the author than he has been given credit for in academic circles.

London's work does not come sprung full-grown out of his head like Athena from Zeus' skull, as H. L. Mencken believes. Mencken writes of London:

> Where did he get his hot artistic passion, his delicate
> feeling for form and color, his extraordinary skill with
> words? The man, in truth, was an instinctive artist of
> a high order, and if ignorance often corrupted his art,
> it only made the fact of his inborn mastery the more
> remarkable. . . . You will never convince me that this
> aesthetic sensitiveness, so rare, so precious, so distinc-
> tively aristocratic, burst into a biogenetic flower on a
> San Francisco sand-lot. There must have been some
> intrusion of an alien and superior strain, some pianis-
> simo fillup from above; there was obviously a great deal
> more to the thing than a routine hatching in low life.

In London's early short stories, the works leading up to the 1903
publication of the culmination of his powers, *The Call of the Wild*,
we find London working through his anxiety over the works
of Nietzsche, Darwin, Herbert Spencer, and Karl Marx. The
stories are a series of imitations, stylistically, formally, and even
in terms of content, of other authors ranging from Walter Scott
to Joseph Conrad. Although London wrote a number of essays
(collected in *The War of the Classes* and *Revolution and Other Essays)*, the essays are more a rehashing of the influences' ideas
than a struggle to overcome those ideas. It is in the short story
form that London attempts to reconcile his varied influences,
and it is in the short story that London confronts, in a literary
format, the canon of intellectual thought with which he grapples.

London's philosophical contradictions, his leanings toward Socialism and Fascism, are paralleled in his aesthetics.
At the same time as London desperately wanted to become a
great literary writer, he despised the literary establishment. He
wanted to be a member of the canon, but he knew in his heart
that he would never be in it truly. It's easy enough for a poor

boy from Oakland to believe that the canon is a club which very few outside the Ivy League are permitted to enter.

The existing canon as we know it, at least the *American* canon, is predominantly white, male, and East Coast. Daisy's voice in *The Great Gatsby* sounds like money, and the canon of American writers *smells* of money.

Kids who went to expensive East Coast private colleges and universities, sent to New York City or Boston to work for a pittance at major publishing houses—working for less than subsistence pay since their rich parents cough up the difference in cash between what they are being paid and what they need to live well—becoming editors of the houses, making the decisions about who gets published and who doesn't—these rich kids become the arbiters of the nation's tastes since they are the gatekeepers of the palace of letters. They read the manuscripts that come into the offices of *The New Yorker* and the *Atlantic* and *The Paris Review*, rejecting works from "the boonies" and sending up to the main editors works with the proper return addresses and pedigrees.

Gather the prominent poets and fictioneers of American history into a room, and do roll call, and about eighty percent of the writers are connected to the Ivy League in some way. Go down the list of poets and it's even more shocking. Minor minds like Edward Hirsch (who received a MacArthur "genius" grant) end up in the canon. Hirsch, of course, went to the University of Pennsylvania and is friends with Harold Bloom, who, I hear, was on the MacArthur committee the year Hirsch was deemed a genius. Flip through a standard anthology of American literature and read the bios. It's truly repellent.

Perhaps it's a good thing that the good folks at the GRE are revamping the exam, although the effect of this revamping will be negligible. For it's almost as if a kid at Harvard can say, "Prof, I want to be a poet when I grow up." Prof:

"Good choice, son! Write some poems, finish the degree, and we'll see to it that you get your little book published, get a fellowship to Yale, and come right on back here when you're done to be a professor." This might sound a bit hyperbolic, but just look at the list! Pearl S. Buck, John Steinbeck, and Sinclair Lewis have Nobel Prizes, for chrissakes—and they don't get taught at the university. It's kind of like the story of Hank Aaron, the baseball player who spent his days in Milwaukee and Atlanta and hit more home runs than Babe Ruth, than Mickey Mantle, than Joe DiMaggio: if Aaron had been a Yankee, he'd have been the most famous ballplayer in history. If only Steinbeck had been a Harvard boy . . .

If only Jack London had been a Harvard boy.

To enter the canon of Western literature should be like becoming a saint of the Catholic Church. To become a saint, a candidate must first perform a miracle before being approved by the high powers of the church. Too many Ivy League writers fail to produce miracles, yet get the nod anyway from the literary powerbrokers. It's a lot more of a miracle nowadays to *not be Ivy* and become a known, influential writer.

We find the staunchest supporters of the canon among scholars with humble roots—Harold Bloom's father was a tailor, Denis Donoghue's father a policeman. Even the echelons of the elite have been invaded, and I suspect that the invaders, out of awe and reverence for the establishment, have ambivalent feelings toward the club they have fought so hard to join. But if their feelings are not ambivalent, it is most likely because they see the canon as the still unattainable emblem of social heights, and worship it as a poor boy in a shack worships a palace in the Oakland hills.

The feelings London has toward the canon, like mine, are contradictory, are emblematic of a lower-class artist's dual-edged pull.

As the poor have entered the ranks of academia, as people from middle- and lower-income families have become professors, the canon has begun to be exposed for the ugly, elitist thing it is. But is it necessarily bad that the canon is elitist? Without it, aesthetic judgment would become so subjective that we would end up reading Chief Seattle instead of Emerson.

The most exciting thing that has happened in the halls of English departments since the critical revolution of the 60s is the current reevaluation of the canon. The poor are slowly infiltrating the ranks of academia, and in revolutionary fashion, they're torching the fortress. When the flames die down and the coals cool, the Great Writers will not be found hanging from the turrets, but they will be keeping some different company.

VII

The Aesthetics of the Poor and the Rich

Fitzgerald says that the rich are not like you and me.

They're not. And they don't write like us, either. Hemingway says, "They have more money." There's more to it.

The art of the rich, of the financially secure, is very different from the art of the poor, of those who've stared into the Abyss.

The aesthetics of writers who fear the Abyss are not embraced by the academic community, and this is why they are largely excluded from the academic version of the canon.

The art produced by the Financially Secure, by those who have never imagined themselves in the Pit, is a quieter kind of art, is an art that strives for aesthetic pleasure above didactic intent. Aesthetics and didacticism both exist in the art of the Financially Secure, but aesthetics comes first, didacticism second.

It's the opposite for those who fear the free-fall into what London calls "the submerged tenth." For artists who fear the fall, who fear that they might find themselves broken and beaten, as a rule didacticism comes first, aesthetics second.

The characters the rich create struggle with their own boredom. Existential angst is the primary focus of most of the work created by the financially stable. The characters in *New Yorker* short stories are much more worried about their deodorant than about their teeth falling out of their heads.

The characters the poor create struggle with death. They tread water in the human cesspool, trying to keep their noses above the feces.

Henry James's Christopher Newman shows up in Paris and is bored. He's looking for things to spend his money on. He's looking for something to pass the time.

Dreiser's Hurstwood moves to New York City with a pile of stolen cash and goes straight down the tubes and ends up hauled away dead with the rest of the garbage.

Gaddis's JR takes the Long Island Railroad into Manhattan, makes money his hobby, and becomes a millionaire and buddies with the president.

Ralph Ellison's Invisible Man shows up in New York City, and he's fighting for his life, for his people, for humanity. He's fighting for the right to exist. And he ends up living in some kind of subterranean hell.

An Updike character rummages through a cedar chest of family mementos in the attic, waxing sentimental about those groovy days of youth.

James Baldwin's characters get hooked on heroin, try to escape the ghetto, struggle against white culture, against each other. They get their balls chopped off and lynched.

Dreiser is admitted into the canon conditionally: we must first accept the "fact" that his prose is inferior. Ellison and Baldwin are admitted conditionally: they are "black" writers. Robert Barltrop notes that, in *Intellectual America*, Oscar Cargill calls London, Upton Sinclair, and Dreiser "witless, heavy-handed progeny" of realists like Frank Norris. Norris, of course, went to Harvard, and write as he might about the poor, he is not one of them. Justice in *The Octopus* prevails. Admittedly, London, Sinclair, and Dreiser don't have the technical skill of Norris, but witless they aren't. What they're likely not to do, however, is, like Norris, kill their villains at the ends of their novels to satisfy some strange Christian code of morality. Norris kills off S. Berman neatly at the end of *The Octopus*, burying him in wheat with a flourish of irony, and it's almost laughable so contrived is it. We'd like to think this is the way the world works, but the truth is that it is not. London, on the other hand, tears sympathetic characters to shreds with the fangs of wolves; Sinclair reduces them to rags; and Dreiser sends them to hell in the despair of suicide. Only recently has the great writer of dread, Edgar Allan Poe, been admitted to the canon, having been considered a writer of scary stories for children for nearly a hundred years. London is not admitted at all, for not only does he not agree with the aesthetics of the rich, he has disdain for them. And they for him. Gordon Mills, in his article "The Transformation of Material in a Mimetic Fiction," writes:

> There is general agreement as to the primary weaknesses in London's fiction: the language is often mawkish; ideas are not always effectively integrated with other elements of a work; in his full-length novels London has trouble with structure and point of view; there is an embarrassing amount of self-dramatizing by the author; and drama tends to collapse into sentimentality. In London's best work, chiefly his stories of the North, these faults are either absent or inconspicuous. But, of course, freedom from such faults is by itself no assurance of greatness; there seems little disposition to claim for London a place among what Clifton Fadiman used to call the major authors.

London is not included among the list of great authors, even though he is the number-one selling American author in the world. His aesthetics don't align with the aesthetics of the academy's notion of "fine art"; he is a barbarian, in their view, a mawkish, clumsy oaf who writes about himself (heaven forbid!). At first glance, it's truly stunning that London is perceived as being a lesser writer than Stephen Crane, whose prose is some of the worst I've ever read. But then, Crane was from the East. He went to an East Coast private university (Syracuse) and was pals with William Dean Howells and Henry James.

Literary aesthetics in America have been dominated by the Ivy League schools to a shocking degree, and consequently American aesthetic principles are primarily set by the writers and critics produced by the Ivy League schools. These principles are the standards of the wealthy, and it should come as no surprise that what we see as "fine" literature in America is that which conveys ease, which conveys a sense of well-being, which follows along the traditional WASP mythology that tells us that everything will work out for the best since God's watching over us. Well, it's easy to see God watching over us if we're rich and don't have to worry about starving or being worked to death in a coal mine. The title of Jack London's volume of short stories, *When God Laughs*, gives us an indication of what those who fear the Abyss think of God.

If a literary artist smacks of considering his art as *work*, if a literary artist is concerned with the poor primarily, eventually that literary artist will be excised from the canon, his work considered the work of a hack of the lower orders, lacking refinement.

It took Dickens nearly a hundred years to be recognized as a literary writer.

Writers from the lower classes want to *change* an unjust world, hence their didacticism.

Writers from the comfortable classes tend to either mock the existing world, or to focus on the dainty, the "smiling" aspects of life, the minutiae, the fine and delicate nuances. There's plenty to be said for this, but note how easy it is to bastardize one of these dainty works, how very little is necessary to turn one of these works into melodrama, as is routinely done when the film industry gets its hands on a Henry James or Jane Austen work.

Note how little *change* is brought about by the writers of the comfortable classes.

Upton Sinclair, on the other hand, altered the way food was inspected and processed in America, and made the strongest Socialist run for the governorship of California the state has known. Steinbeck brought worldwide attention to the poor of California. The writers of the Harlem Renaissance were the precursors to the Civil Rights movement. Alice Walker, John Edgar Wideman, and Toni Morrison have brought literary dignity and pride and interest to a culture that had all but given up on literature.

What did Eliot change in the world at large?

Have John Ashbery and Wallace Stevens altered the minds of anyone but other snotty poets?

Emily Dickinson's biggest contribution to the world is that she gave subsequent poets license to be unreadably obscure.

What does Henry James really *do*, other than provide aesthetic pleasure to readers with graduate degrees in English literature?

What we consider fine literature is that which comes closest to the Wilde/Pater Oxford-bred notion of Art for Art's Sake. Keep politics out. Write, as William Dean Howells would have us do, about the "smiling aspects of life."

Writers who feel themselves teetering on the edge of poverty generally don't have much regard for the "smiling aspects of life."

James McClintock writes that

the Howellsian sense of the "average" or the "commonplace" . . . were hateful words to London. The experiences London used as the stuff for his fiction had sprung from his lower class existence and included the crude, the violent and the sordid, all "average" to him, but not to Howells who assumed the middle class American as the norm for perception. Literature written from a Howellsian perspective bored London; it was bloodless. He wanted his stories to "live and spout blood and spirit and beauty and fire and glamor."

The "Howellsian sense," of course, has proven to be law in terms of defining the canon of American writers who wrote during Howells' dictatorship. Middle-class life—the tedium and angst of meaninglessness so often glorified on the pages of *The New Yorker*, *Atlantic Monthly*, *Harper's*, and *Esquire*—is the model of excellence today as it was a hundred years ago when Daisy Miller paraded around Washington Square like an airhead bimbo. James McClintock, in *Jack London's Strong Truths*, writes:

> The predominance of death and violence in London's short stories disturbed some of the early critics who rejected him as a sensationalist, and very few later critics have realized that through violence London was probing experiences neglected by his contemporaries. Moreover, he probed with an integrity, sincerity and insight rarely associated with him. . . . Death and violence serve as an "initiatory rite into manhood." And "manhood" can be more fully understood as a full awareness of the individual's participation with the unknowable universe that has an anti-human malignancy as one of its components. The act of killing is a concession to the unknowable and an admission that man has an internal counterpart to destructive natural forces.

Death and violence aren't "initiatory rites into manhood," and murder isn't "a concession to the unknowable." Death and violence are facts to someone with a lower-class upbringing. By the time an Oakland kid is on his own in the world, he has seen friends, family members, neighbors, and random people on the streets beaten, raped, murdered, tortured, abused, maimed, literally ripped to shreds by other human beings. One of my best friends in high school, Karl Slominsky, made the mistake of looking with a sneer at a group of Mexicans standing outside a 7-11 convenience store. For his indiscretion, he was stabbed repeatedly, and then chained to the rear bumper of their car. They dragged him six miles. There wasn't much left of him except the torso. Body parts were collected into bags as evidence. The Mexicans were minors, and so sent to juvenile hall instead of prison. When they were released as they reached legal age, they disappeared, one by one. Everyone in the neighborhood knew what was happening—Karl's older brothers were taking care of business, as was right and proper. This is the way life works among the lower classes. In the lower classes, which are much larger than Howells and the literary establishment would have us believe, death and violence are not aberrations. They are the norm.

Jack London doesn't follow the law of Dean Howells. In a letter to his longtime editor at Macmillan, George P. Brett, dated March 7, 1907, London writes:

> I am willing to grant the chance that I am wholly wrong in believing that sincerity and truthfulness constitute my big asset. I am willing to grant the chance that I am wholly mistaken in my reasoning. Nevertheless, I look back on my life and draw one great generalization: IT WAS MY REFUSAL TO TAKE CAUTIOUS AD-VICE THAT MADE ME. At the very beginning, had I taken the advice of the magazine editors, I'd have

been swiftly made into a failure. McClure's Magazine gave me $125 per month, and held the bread-and-butter lash over me. Phillips said, "Write such and such stories for our magazine. Quit writing the stories you are writing." In short, he wanted to make me take the guts and backbone out of my stories; wanted me to make an eunuch of myself; wanted me to write petty, smug, complacent bourgeois stories; wanted me to enter the ranks of clever mediocrity and there to pander to the soft, fat, cowardly bourgeois instincts.

His contempt for frilly stories in which nothing is truly at stake—nothing weighty, at any rate—is utter. Fiction that is gutless and that panders to the middle- and upper-class tastes of the rich is fiction that betrays the great horde of humanity who slave their lives away keeping the wealthy fat and happy. London writes in a letter, "I consider the primary weakness in the average stories and verses of the younger writers to be lack of guts and plenitude of conventionality." What London means by "guts" is pretty close to what Emerson means when he says in "Self-Reliance," "Familiar as the voice of the mind is to each, the highest merit we ascribe to Moses, Plato and Milton is that they set at naught books and traditions, and spoke not what men, but what *they* thought." D. H. Lawrence, a writer with working-class roots, says, "Be still when you have nothing to say; when genuine passion moves you, say what you've got to say, and say it hot." Saying what one *truly* thinks, though, is itself problematic, for it necessitates a delving into the soul that can result in the kind of horror that Kurtz finds himself experiencing at the end of *Heart of Darkness*. The self is not necessarily a pretty thing, as London so aptly demonstrates in his Northland stories. Catering to the tastes of the rabble, a writer who doesn't have the courage to "set at naught books and traditions" is odious to London, who sees the rabble as the gang of bourgeois editors and critics and professors and other purveyors of the tastes, both moral and aesthetic, of the day. London says in one of his letters that a writer should

> not be a slave to convention; that he build not as his fathers built; that he think for himself, and that he accept truth wherever he finds it, and not because it is garbed in fine linen and goes prancing around in an automobile or a church pulpit, a university-chair, or an editor's sanctum. In short, my hint is that the young writer who expects to become a great writer must think beyond the mass of his fellow-creatures, and that the mass of his fellow-creatures thinks along the same lines as think the preachers, the professors, and the editors.

London's open contempt for the editors, professors, and preachers is a product of the mind-set of a poor boy. He sees the upper echelon of society as the enemy, as the oppressor, as that group of people which actively strives to keep the tastes and needs of the lower classes not only in check, but forever out of the public eye. The upper classes are the enemy. In an open letter to the laborers of the country, London, in support of Upton Sinclair's *The Jungle*, writes that the book

> depicts what our country really is, the home of oppression and injustice, a nightmare of misery, an inferno of suffering, a human hell, a jungle of wild beasts.
>
> And take notice and remember, comrades, this book is straight proletarian. And straight proletarian it must be throughout. It is written by an intellectual proletarian. It is written for the proletariat. It is published by a proletarian publishing house. It is to be read by the proletariat. And depend upon it, if it is not circulated

> by the proletariat it will not be circulated at all. In
> short, it must be a supreme proletarian effort.
>   Remember, this book must go out in the face of
> the enemy. No capitalist publishing house would
> dare to publish it. It will be laughed at—some; jeered
> at—some; abused—some; but most of all, worst of all,
> the most dangerous treatment it will receive is that of
> silence. For that is the way of capitalism.
>   Comrades, do not forget the conspiracy of silence.

The rich, the fat, the complacent—they are the enemy. And
of course, the worst the enemy can do to a literary work that
challenges their aesthetics and morality is to ignore that work,
to greet it with silence, to refuse to review it, to deny it a place
in the circuit of influence dictated by the East Coast literary
establishment.

And it tends to be with silence that works which come
from the lower classes are met. Since the nation's literary tastes
have been and continue to be set by the wealth and comfort of
the Ivy Mafia, it makes perfect sense that a Nobel Prize winner
like John Steinbeck would be excluded from the anthologies
and the literature survey courses, and young undergraduates
struggling to escape the depths of society through attending
community colleges are instead given doses of Henry James
(Harvard), T. S. Eliot (Harvard), Wallace Stevens (Harvard),
John Ashbery (Harvard), Gaddis (Harvard), Elizabeth Bishop
(Vassar—taught at Harvard), Robert Bly (Harvard), and so
forth ad nauseam.

Imagine: the student is a first-generation college student,
and the teacher explains that "The Beast in the Jungle" is included in the anthology and "To Build a Fire" is not because
James *hides* his didacticism, *hides* his ideas behind complex
prose, and London is too obvious, and therefore inferior. I've
seen these students trying to slug through Gertrude Stein

(Radcliffe/Harvard), seen a teacher try to explain to them that this! this *Melanctha* is the true stuff of literature! It's a hard one to swallow. I've seen the impenetrable Pynchon (Cornell) held up as the example of literary greatness to students like Michael's flaming sword guarding the entrance of Eden: "You, *beast*, are *not* allowed to enter."

The students are taught that art is for the refined mind, that as Wilde says, "The only excuse for making a useless thing is that one admires it intensely," and "All art is quite useless." Far be it that art serve a *purpose*! If it serves a purpose, it smacks of the lower classes, of the brute element, and that will not do if we are to create a *proper* aesthetic standard. Rilke's *Letters to a Young Poet* is a perennial crowd-pleaser for aesthetes, even though it is not much more than a pale imitation of Walter Pater's ideas in his "Conclusion" to *The Renaissance*, while Upton Sinclair's brilliant little book, *Letters to Judd, An American Workingman*, is long out of print and cast away with the rest of the books of the poor and well-intentioned. In it Sinclair does not parrot the party line, writing, for instance:

> We know by now what the word "privilege" means. Hundreds of thousands of people do not have to do useful labor in our society; they draw off the profits of other people's labor, and the good things of life flow to them in a stream so great as sometimes to overwhelm them. And this flow is guaranteed them for life, and to their descendants to the end of time. All our political teachings, all our economic calculations, are based upon the idea that this state of affairs is permanent. . . .

From the side of power and cash, however, Pater writes in his "Conclusion," "For art comes to you proposing frankly to give nothing but the highest quality to your moments as they pass, and simply for those moments' sake"—and the power of the academy, of the reigning forces of intellectual standards, backs him. Even the comfortable Emerson thinks that literature should be a bit rough and rugged. In "American Scholar," he writes:

> We have listened too long to the courtly muses of Europe. The spirit of the American freeman is already suspected to be timid, imitative, tame. Public and private avarice make the air we breathe thick and fat. The scholar is decent, indolent, complaisant. See already the tragic consequence. The mind of this country, taught to aim at low objects, eats upon itself. There is no work for any but the decorous and the complaisant.

London could have written these lines himself. But decency ruled the day not only in Emerson's time, and not only in London's time, but now as well. We are taught that art should be for art's sake only.

And this makes sense, since it is the elite class which sets the standards. If art is for art's sake only, then it's pretty damned easy to abjure social responsibility and to condemn didactic work as inferior, as inferior work produced by inferior writers from the inferior classes, as sour grapes from the pens of the poor: "Yes," the guardians of the aesthetics of the rich would seem to say, "the poor are sincere, but surely one notes the lack of *intellectual acuity*, the lack of *aesthetic principles*, the gaping holes in the poor writers' educations."

The contradictions we find in London's social philosophies are the same contradictions we find in his aesthetics, in the tools through which he delivers his social philosophies. He wants to be an artist of the first order, a "made" man in the Ivy Mafia, but he also wants to be a writer of the people.

The two goals have rarely coincided in American literary history.

We can find an example of London's contradictory aesthetic stances in a single paragraph; he writes, in response to a query from the editors of *Editor*, the following:

> I should advise the young story-writer to leave the old masters in literature alone, if he wishes to sell stories to the present-day magazines. I should advise the young story-writer to study the stories in the current magazines; in this case, if he has anything in him he will succeed in selling stories to the modern editors. But I must append this warning: HE WILL SUCCEED WITH THE EDITORS OF TO-DAY; BUT IN THE CENTURIES TO COME HE WILL NOT HIMSELF BE ACCREDITED A MASTER IN LITERATURE.

He says *not* to read great literature, to only study contemporary successful writers, and at the same time he says that this act will doom the writer to the literary dust-bin, to historical oblivion. But London also believes that the great masters *should* be studied, and throughout his collected letters he refers to the great masters. London knew his literature.

Writers who come from the cellar of society read the great writers no matter which class the great writers happen to come from. Writers come from all classes. In "On the Level of Desire" Donald Barthelme writes,

> The four social classes under late capitalism are
> > Artists
> > Rich people
> > The middle class
> > Poor people

—this being the order and rank of precedence.

As the dominant class (morally/intellectually speaking), artists have a clear social responsibility to care for and nurture the three lower classes. This is not by any means their primary responsibility, which is of course to art, but neither is it a negligible one.

Artists come from any of the three "lower" classes, and exist as a separate class unto themselves.* Barthelme seems to think that once a person has entered the "artist" class, that person leaves his lower-class roots behind in the service of art, which is the primary responsibility of the artist. This is the typical party line of the Financially Stable, of which Barthelme was a member.

Vladimir Nabokov, born of an aristocratic family, writes, "A work of art has no importance whatever to society. It is only important to the individual, and only the individual reader is important to me. I don't give a damn for the group, the community, the masses, and so forth." This is what we'd expect to hear from an aristocrat. He might as well have gone to Yale. He taught at Cornell—Ivy, of course.

When a lower- or working-class person sallies forth into the world of letters, a world historically sponsored by aristocracies and their progenies and variants, he makes himself acquainted with the canon, with literary history. He strives to emulate the great writers of history. In doing so, it is only natural that he be swayed by the aesthetics of the ruling classes which fostered and nourished the great writers of Western history and culture. The aesthetics of the rich, from Aristotle and Longinus through Sidney and Kant and Derrida have a narcotic allure. "Open sesame!" we say to the boulder, and if it rolls away from the entrance to the cave, we find the golden riches within. The aesthetics of the rich promise riches.

So a writer from the lower or working class feels the pull of the aesthetics of the rich. Not only have the aesthetics of the rich been honed and shaped and made precise and intricate through two thousand years of cultural and intellectual lathe work, not only have the aesthetics of the rich a religiously sacred canon and an austere tradition of mutual congratulation, but it's the aesthetics of the rich which, to use contemporary examples, get you a MacArthur "genius" grant, which get you a chair teaching creative writing at Columbia, which get you a buck and a half a word in *The New Yorker*, which get you into the American Academy of Arts and Letters. And not only that, but the rich, quite simply, write better. Their skills are honed since birth, tutored and privately educated into the flesh and blood and bones. Growing up around literate parents, with books in the house, surrounded by like children and associates, with college an assumption and not a fairy tale, the educated classes simply have more facility with the language. There's really not much question that James can outwrite London any day of the week. It would be laughable to compare the stylistic perfection of John Updike with the clumsiness of Dreiser, whose mother was illiterate and whose father kept the family in poverty.

Brilliant style is one of the hallmarks of the rich. Consequently, the lack of a brilliant style is considered the mark of an inferior writer. The almost fanatical emphasis on style is an upper-class affectation consequent of having no substance about which to write.

Oscar Wilde writes, "In all unimportant matters, style, not sincerity, is the essential. In all important matters, style, not sincerity, is the essential." And: "Only the great masters of style ever succeed in being obscure."

Schopenhauer, however, offers a contrary view in "On Books and Writing": "Obscurity and vagueness of expression is always and everywhere a very bad sign: for in 99 cases out of 100 it derives from vagueness of thought, which in turn comes from an original incongruity in the thought itself, and thus from its falsity." And: "The first rule, indeed by itself virtually a sufficient condition for good style, is to have something to say."

Style, according to Schopenhauer, is the ability to express content clearly. For Wilde, style is the ability to cloud and confuse. Wilde's assessment rules the day in the elite canon of Western culture, hence the worship of such writers as Stevens, Dickinson, Joyce, Proust, James, Stein, and Pound.

Schopenhauer writes,

> An *affected* writer is like a man who dresses up so as not to be confused and confounded with the mob [like Oscar Wilde], a danger which a gentleman, however ill-clad, never runs. As a certain overdressing and *tiré à quatre épingles* thus betrays the plebeian, so an affected style betrays the commonplace mind.

I don't claim Proust, Joyce, and company to be commonplace minds. I do, however, question their respective entourages, their literary groupies.

What, for God's sake, *are* Pound's *Cantos*? How many languages is a person supposed to master before he's permitted into the sanctum sanctorum of Pound's work?

Pound's *Cantos* are poems for the rich. They, therefore, are considered to be high art, to be literature. For no one I know personally can read them and honestly say they understand them. If they're beyond the typical PhD in this country, they must be something really special.

Conversely, since a person can read Jack London and understand what he's saying the first time around, he is relatively simple. Therefore, the guardians at the gate would say, his work is not literature. His work is inferior on the grounds of its accessibility.

Notes

* It is interesting to note how D. H. Lawrence, a writer from the working class, arrives at a conclusion similar to that of Barthelme. Lawrence, in his essay "Autobiographical Sketch," writes the following:

> The answer, as far as I can see, has something to do with class. Class makes a gulf, across which all the best human flow is lost. It is not exactly the triumph of the middle classes that has made the deadness, but the triumph of the middle-class *thing*.
>
> As a man from the working class, I feel that the middle class cut off some of my vital vibration when I am with them. I admit them charming and educated and good people often enough. *But they just stop some part of me from working.* Some part has to be left out.
>
> Then why don't I live with my working people? Because their vibration is limited in another direction. They are narrow, but still fairly deep and passionate, whereas the middle class is broad and shallow and passionless. Quite passionless. At the best they substitute affection, which is the great middle-class positive emotion.
>
> But the working class is narrow in outlook, in prejudice, and narrow in intelligence. This again makes a prison. One can belong absolutely to no class.

VIII

STYLE AND STORY

A writer who is complex stylistically is favored in academia over a writer who tells good stories but who lacks stylistic complexity.

Good stories that can be enjoyed by the hoi polloi, by definition, then, are not art. For the hoi polloi, according to academics, are incapable of enjoying fine art.

Thomas Pynchon is preferable to John Steinbeck. William Gaddis is preferable to Sinclair Lewis. Gertrude Stein is preferable to Jack London.

Literary fiction in the 20th century has largely been an abandonment of the notion of the story, a ripping apart, a vivisection of the archetypal structure of a narrative. From the experiments of James in such later novels as *The Ambassadors*, *The Wings of the Dove*, and *The Golden Bowl*, to the works of the modernists—Gertrude Stein's *The Making of Americans*, Dos Passos' *USA*, Faulkner's *Go Down, Moses*, Joyce and Beckett and Woolf in Europe—to the assault on the notion of story waged by the postmodernists, Barth's novels and short stories, Robert Coover's *Pricksongs and Descants*, the works of Fiction Collective writers Ronald Sukenick (*Up, Out, 98.6*, and *Long Talking Bad Conditions Blues*), Raymond Federman (*Take It or Leave It*), Steve Katz (*The Confessions of Peter Prince, Moving Parts*), Donald Barthelme's short stories and his *Snow White* and *The Dead Father*, the works of the Latin American writers Cabrera Infante (*Three Trapped Tigers* and *Infante's Inferno*), Julio Cortázar (*Hopscotch*), and Manuel Puig (*Eternal Curse on the Reader of These Pages*)—literary fiction has foregone the traditional notion of the narrative, has pushed the outside limits of the forms of the novel and the short story. This tendency has devalued the work of storytellers whose style has not kept pace with their storytelling abilities.

But we're still a nation that consumes stories, yarns, jokes, personal narratives, and movies. The movies are the most lucrative venue for a writer in the history of mankind: write one movie, become a millionaire. Sell the movie rights and, if the thing goes into even one stage of production, about three hundred grand comes your way. We love stories, and we're willing to pay people who will tell them to us. And we're not all too worried about the word-by-word delivery of the story, either—no. What we're concerned with is if the story "holds our attention," if we can "relate to" the story, to use the phrases my undergraduates most commonly employ when deciding whether or not "The Dead" by Joyce is as good a story as, say, "To Build a Fire" by Jack London. London always wins, because the students don't really give a hoot whether or not London was experimenting with point of view, whether or not he was discovering stream-of-consciousness narrative, whether or not he'd perfected the delivery of the literary epiphany.

There is no reason to condescend to the great supposedly unwashed undergraduate population. These students are, after all, the elite, the educated, and though perhaps not intending to be students of literature, they are the educated, literate class, the future upon which literature, if it is to continue to exist at all, depends. So when my students say they'd rather read Poe than Gertrude Stein, when they throw their books down in disgust over *Finnegans Wake* and cheer when they're reading James Fenimore Cooper, call me a simpleton, scorn my lack of refinement and culture, but I not only *understand* my undergraduates' point of view, I agree with it.

At the same time, though, I loathe my undergraduates' point of view, and see it as the product of a lack of education, as a sign of ignorance.

Jack London faces this dilemma his entire writing career. In order to reach the work beasts, in order to alter the consciousness of the class of people he calls his "comrades," he must write work they can understand, work they can read and comprehend. By doing so, however, he assures himself that he will not become part of the elite, part of the East Coast literary establishment and therefore part of the canon of writers respected by the dictators of the academy.

If he writes for "the people," he is damned by the Ivies.

If he writes for the Ivies, although he might enter the almighty canon, the people of his class will remain forever wallowing in their ignorance and drudgery and slavery to the capitalist classes.

Richard Brodhead writes, in his book *Cultures of Letters*:

> The history of literary access, conceived as the history of the processes by which literary writing has had different cultural places made for it, and so has had different groups placed in different proximities to it; the history of access, conceived at the same time as the history of the acts—successful, failed, and partially achieved—by which potential authors have made themselves into authors within the opportunities and obstructions of particular social situations: this is the history we need to begin to compose if we would understand the relation of the whole of humanity to the whole field of letters.

Gaining access to the highest levels of the American literary establishment is indeed a difficult piece of work, and usually entails hobnobbing with either Ivy-League connected people, or New Yorkers. To gain entrance, a writer must subscribe to the aesthetics of the elite power brokers. This creates a problem for the writer who hails from an impoverished background, and is doubly difficult if the writer does not have access to New York or Boston.

I gained access to the literary elite by spending my retirement savings—$45,000—and going another $35,000 into debt. I had to buy my way into the club.

When I first began writing fiction, over twenty years ago, my goal was to write novels that both my professors and the men on the construction site alongside me would enjoy, the professors for the literary merit of the book—its style—and the construction workers for the power of the story I was telling, for its social relevance. I wanted the professors to have compassion for the lower classes, and the construction workers to have an appreciation of artistic beauty. I swore that I'd never use a word in a work of fiction that needed to be looked up in a dictionary. It would be a betrayal of my people. I wrote my books, social novels which attempted to follow the dictates of the elite aesthetics while preaching my soapbox complaints, and sent them into the void—to New York City—where scores of gatekeepers simply wrote on the cover of my manuscript box, "Return to Sender—Not Reading at this Time." I was, after all, just a Texan, and though I was Editor of the literary magazine of the University of Houston, *Gulf Coast*, I was a bumpkin from the provinces. I finally had to enroll in a private, East Coast university, move to New York City, become an editor of a New York-based literary journal, and go to the right parties. With the address and pedigree change, I won an NEA grant using a piece of fiction that had been denied an NEA grant several times before, got published in the nation's premier literary journals, and got one of my books (one of the same books that no one would read when I lived in Texas) published by a major New York publisher. The book, although acceptable enough by the established to merit publication, is nonetheless a social novel, an exposé on the ill-treatment of the poor in Oakland, California. I'm trying to help the poor while pleasing the rich.

London seems to have had the same goal: he wanted to write for both the working class and for the elite. He wanted to write for the elite without betraying the workers, and for the workers without becoming a laughingstock in the eyes of the elite. London is still being written about in academia, and his collected letters and stories issued on Stanford University Press attest to the fact that the academy, albeit perhaps grudgingly, accepts him. He is one of the very few American writers of literary repute whose works are purchased and read by both the college educated and the non-college educated. The finest fusion of London's double-edged aesthetics is found in *The Call of the Wild.*

London's social books, *The People of the Abyss* and *The Iron Heel*, books he wrote in furies of passion for the lower classes, for the workers, for the people from which he came, were commercial failures as well as aesthetic failures. The books didn't sell well, and they were as poorly written, if not even worse, than the most vile of his works, books such as *Burning Daylight* and *Smoke Bellew.* The people he wanted to help didn't read relatively complex works. The people who did read complex works, aside from disliking the rotten prose, didn't like the subject matter—the Socialist stance. It was like the speech London made in New York City, addressing what Philip Foner calls "an exclusive group of extremely wealthy men and women." London told them:

You have been entrusted with the world; you have muddled and mismanaged it. You are incompetent, despite all your boastings. A million years ago the caveman, without tools, with small brain, and with nothing but the strength of his body, managed to feed his wife and children, so that through him the race survived. You, on the other hand, armed with all the modern means of production, multiplying the productive capacity of the cavemen a million times—you are incompetents and muddlers, you are unable to secure to millions even the paltry amount of bread that would sustain their physical life. You have mismanaged the world, and it shall be taken from you.

Who will take it from you? We will! And who are we? We are seven million revolutionists and we are everywhere growing. And we want all you have! Look at us! We are strong! Consider our hands! They are strong hands, and even now they are reaching forth for all you have, and they will take it, take it by the power of their strong hands; take it from your feeble grasp. Long or short though the time may be, that time is coming. The army is on the march, and nothing can stop it, that you can stop it is ludicrous. It wants nothing less than all you have, and it will take it; you are incompetent and will have to surrender to the strong. We are the strong, and in that day we shall give you an exhibition of power such as your feeble brains never dreamed the world contained.

He was, of course, biting the hand that fed him, for it wasn't the poor that were providing his royalty checks. But these are not the words of an armchair Socialist. They are the words of a man who truly hates the rich, even as he becomes one of them, even as he lectures at Harvard and Yale. London's aesthetics are not confused here, nor are his philosophies. If the country isn't going to be a Socialist one, then he's a fool to wallow with the poor with whom he was raised. Just because he is no longer poor, however, does not mean that he does not despise the system of which he is a part. What's different about a poor boy done good is that unlike a person born into wealth, the person born into poverty despises the wealth he is forced either to never have or to accumulate through capitalist, and therefore brutal, means.

And so London in his work forgoes the niceties of style and concentrates on the story he wants to tell, on the lesson he wants to preach. Style is secondary to the content he wishes to deliver. And when we think about it, we cannot but admit that fiction is first and foremost a narrative event, a tale, a yarn with a beginning, middle, and end. Not until the beginning of the demise of poetry—brought on partially by the Romantics and their abandonment of form, partially by the advances in the printing press which made books cheap and readily available, and largely by an increasingly literate and semiliterate society—did matters of style begin to become equal to, if not more important than, the notion that the story was the most important element of a work of fiction. Samuel Richardson certainly did not have style as his primary concern when he wrote *Pamela* and *Clarissa* for the periodicals, and Daniel Defoe cannot be praised for his style. Plot was the crucial element of what we consider fiction. In the middle of the 19th century, when poetry began to lose its stronghold as the pinnacle of literary endeavors, novelists and their critics began the slow process of seeking the same freight and precision of language in fiction that had come to be a matter of course in poetry. Poe's dictates in his "Review of Hawthorne's *Twice-Told Tales*" exemplify this new set of criteria, criteria which had become implicit by the time of the Modernists, when writers such as Gertrude Stein and James Joyce, Marcel Proust and Malcolm Lowry all but abandoned plot in favor of style.

With this new (and continuing) emphasis on style, writers such as Jack London, James Fenimore Cooper, and Theodore Dreiser—storytellers—would seem to suffer.

But in the long run they won't. Story transcends time, whereas style becomes merely an idiosyncrasy of era. Story is translatable, whereas style is not.

The mark of a fine fiction style is that it is transparent, or, if not transparent, then irrelevant. A truly accomplished fiction style does not call attention to itself, but instead vanishes in service of the story. Style will always become dated. A great story will not.

A *great* style, however, is one that is translatable. It is always a by-product of content, a means through which content is delivered most effectively.

When the Chinese produce a Shakespeare play, they produce it for the story, not for the style. Shakespeare in Chinese is still Shakespeare.

Since literary fiction writers have all but abandoned the idea of writing good, solid *stories*, the population at large, including most of the educated population, prefers movies to written fiction. Movies deliver the stories modern people crave. Ask any American how many movies he watches compared to how many novels he reads, and unless that American is a literature professor, a writer of novels, or a liar, chances are that that American watches more movies, the short stories of today.

In London's day, there weren't movies. People read short stories in lieu of going to the cinema. What London attempted in his best work was to bridge the gap between high literature and low literature, to write work that would endure *and* sell. Some of our best filmmakers do the same today: the Cohn brothers, Martin Scorsese, Francis Ford Coppola. It's what Hitchcock managed to do in his time. John Huston directed films that common folks wanted to see and film students study today.

Modernist fiction writers and the rise of film have killed literary fiction in this country. Good riddance. What was once an event—the daily reading of stories for millions of Americans in magazines such as *Colliers, The Atlantic, The Saturday Evening Post, Overland Monthly, Cosmopolitan, Scribner's Magazine,* and scores of other slicks—has now been relegated to a position akin to that of poetry. Let's face it: the only people in America who read poetry are literature professors and poets. Likewise, the only readers of literary fiction are lit professors and fiction writers. Consequently, the writers of fiction in contemporary America have—understandably—abandoned the college-educated, literate, but not *literary,* market, writing not to entertain, but instead to win prizes, to secure tenure, to get published in journals which, if they pay at all, pay minuscule amounts and are read by less than 10,000 readers (*The Georgia Review*'s circulation is about 6000; *The Southern Review*'s, 3000; and the circulation of *The Iowa Review* is less than 1500—and Iowa's writing program is considered the best in the land, its journal considered among the best showcases for contemporary American fiction). The slicks that publish fiction—*The Atlantic, The New Yorker, Harper's, Esquire, GQ,* and *Redbook*—publish it as a sentimental concession, and rarely even feature ads in the margins of the stories since fiction doesn't sell advertising space. *The New Yorker* often doesn't even run fiction in an issue, and when they do, the story is usually less than 3000 words—a far cry from the days when they ran an entire novel, *Snow White,* by Donald Barthelme. In Jack London's time, he was getting a thousand dollars per story, contracted, for instance, by *Cosmopolitan* to write a story per month for a year—a thousand bucks per story.

Rent in a working-class neighborhood in Oakland at the turn of the century was between ten and twenty dollars per month; a thousand dollars would pay the rent for about four years. There is no venue for short fiction today that matches those of London's time.

Literary fiction these days, however, deserves low payment. It has marginalized itself, and limps along effete and sissified in the realm of "pure art," of "art for art's sake," of, finally and deservedly, obscurity. Mention the names of Mary Robison, Barry Hannah, Jamaica Kincaid, Tracy Daugherty, Bobbie Ann Mason, Padgett Powell, Ann Beattie, Tobias Wolfe, Amy Hempl, Donald Barthelme, Robert Coover, John Hawkes, Angela Carter, Robert Stone, Robert Taylor, Chris Offutt, or any of the other "stars" of the contemporary short story to the average educated American—and I mean people with college degrees and even graduate degrees—and, unless in the unlikely event he was taught the author in a sophomore survey course or he is an English major, likely he will never have heard of the author. Literary fiction is dead.

It deserves to be so.

Literary fiction writers, following the example of poets, have contempt for the American populace at large.*

We hear a lot of wailing from academic critics about the dismal state of affairs in the contemporary literary scene. Much of the wailing is about the rotten poetry, and we really can't argue with the critics on this point. Poetry has indeed declined into a special, narcissistic, private place. It is a rare poet indeed who is not a member of the academy—university instructed, creative writing program trained, sucking the teat of the academy. And a read of contemporary poetry's greatest hits reveals this influence: the poets have their trendy academic stances—Queer Poets, Lesbian Poets, Minority Poets, L-A-N-G-U-A-G-E Poets, Poets of Social Conscience, Marxist Poets, and so forth. An anthology of critical poses aligned with the Big Guns of poetry would be revealing, for the correspondences would not fail to reveal the academic programme behind nearly every poet in the contemporary "canon," canon now meaning—instead of that group of writers whose work creates the Bloomian "anxiety of influence"—that group of poets which controls creative writing programs, literary periodicals (note how many of the current journals are run by practicing poets), and award-granting institutions.

And the work which is not blatantly academic in nature is, for the most part, sentimental tripe. The slush piles of the quarterlies are inundated with poems that feature in the first line "My" and a reference to a blood relation—"Grandmother," "Grandfather," "Mother," "Father," "Uncle," "Ex-Step-Foster-Brother," "Wife." God has long been a musty corpse, and we've been making gods of the ninnies who reared us. Any person who has influenced what we euphemistically call our "thoughts" is relegated Olympian status. And more often than not, the godlike relative's body parts (usually digits) become synecdoches for the cosmos: "My grandmother's fingers," "My Uncle Larry's probing thumb," "My father's hairy toes," and then a leap to a trite memory or a metaphysical epiphany of the lowest order. The Wordsworthian and Whitmanian godlike first-person has been replaced with a sobbing Oprah-gallery sniveler. Gone are the philosophers and the lovers, gone are the splendors of bold assertion and daring generalization. Gone, sadly, are ideas. What's left in the great bulk of modern poetry is sappy sentimentalism, gimmicky trope games, and academic posturing.

Likewise, fiction has slouched, smelling of health-food-store bulk-rate spice and herb remedies and New Age apothecary's powders and nutmeg-sprinkled espresso. Smug writers of existential boredom and trust-fund anxious scribblers of myopic self-pity predominate the slicks, and the quarterlies are become swamped with the stewing miasma of confessional fiction and—even worse—the "personal essay" craze, pseudo-academically engineered by failed fiction writers in creative writing programs as a slightly more sophisticated version of talk-show blubbering and wallowing. Literary fiction writers are following in the cloven hoofsteps of the poets, taking refuge in the academic sty, rooting around with their snouts for tenure. Like poets, literary fiction writers have contempt and disdain for common folks. Entertainment is for the masses, and the masses are, by definition, dullards.

Jack London is often criticized for his work as a hack, for the stories and novels he wrote for the ignoble purpose of making a buck, of making a living in capitalist America.

Remember: he wrote in the days before writers landed university chairs and were free to write books no one would ever read or give a damn about. A writer like Gilbert Sorrentino at Stanford—longtime head fiction writer in the prestigious Stegner Fellow program—whose books appear on small presses and don't even get reviewed, much less read—would have had to write, in London's time, something people would actually have wanted to read, had he wanted to make a living. His "critically acclaimed" book, *Mulligan Stew*, nearly as unreadable as *Finnegans Wake*, might have landed him a university position, but in times of old, it would have landed him a swift kick in the rear toward poverty. San Diego State University's Harold Jaffe, whose books are aggressively unreadable and glib, would have been selling tortillas from a cart had he lived in London's time. Imagine writers like Raymond Federman, John Gorman, Stuart Dybeck, Clarence Major, and literally thousands of other "writers," the university teat withdrawn, having to make a living by their cigar-butt pens. Imagine any American university poet having to make a living on his poetry alone. Even the patronized poets of old had to please someone: the university writers of today, once tenured, have absolutely no obligation to please anyone.

Of course some might argue that this is all to the good, that we've entered truly into an age of Art for Art's Sake, with the writers at long last unshackled from the chains of capitalistic servitude and free, finally, to create pure, unadulterated Art.

But pure, unadulterated art—for whom is this stuff written? If only the highly trained professional reader can read the fiction or poetry, if only a few hundred people on the planet can understand the book, what—and I mean this truly—is the point of creating that book other than to be a snob?

Those who rue the disgust many younger academics have for the traditional notion of the canon may have a point in asking this question: What is the purpose of "art for art's sake" if no one can understand that art?

High art in Western culture has gradually moved from the public arena to a very limited private club.

In what we call "High Art" in literary fiction, the emphasis is on style, not content; delivery, not story.

Jack London's work suffers because it does not subscribe to the modern literary emphasis on style.

Notes

* Two valuable books on contemporary fiction which provide interesting overviews are John W. Aldridge's *The American Novel and the Way We Live Now* (1983) and his *Talents and Technicians: Literary Chic and the New Assembly-Line Fiction* (1992). With passion and occasionally with insight, Aldridge evaluates the state of contemporary fiction. Although he would benefit from perusing the literary journals a bit, and although he seems plagued with the lazy scholar's disease of referring only to *The New Yorker* and *The Atlantic Monthly* and *Harper's* when searching for contemporary work, his insights into several classes of contemporary fiction merit consideration. If nothing else, Aldridge has the guts to make generalizations that are not afraid of being polemic.

IX

DIDACTICISM IN LITERATURE

Not only is London's style out of style, but his brand of didacticism is as well. The role of didacticism in literature is problematic. Writers instruct writers not to be didactic, not to let the characters be mouthpieces for their ideas. Jack London is insistent when he writes critical pieces on the writing of fiction that writers should not be didactic. When he writes to Cloudesley Johns, he tells him the same thing: "Don't tell the readers your philosophy." In writing workshops across the country today, the writer/professors tell their students/budding writers the cliché, "Show, don't tell." Everywhere we turn, writers are told not to be didactic, not to tell the reader their ideas, but instead to *demonstrate*, to *dramatize* their ideas through the actions of the characters.

This all sounds fine, in theory. If our fiction and poetry were larded up with the ideas of the writers, if our fiction and poetry were nothing more than a bunch of narrators and characters standing around pontificating about their theories, what we'd have would not be poetry and fiction, but merely essays posing as fiction, essays posing as poetry, essays posing as drama. We'd have works as overtly didactic as *The People of the Abyss* and *The Iron Heel*, and the pleasure factor of reading literature would likely be reduced dramatically. If our writers were to pontificate endlessly, either in the guise of a persona like Ernest Everhard of *The Iron Heel* or from the mouth of a character like Wolf Larsen of *The Sea Wolf*, then our literature would be tedious stuff.

The practice of studying literature, however, becomes curious indeed. For in study after study, book after book, lecture after lecture, what we find is that professors of literature, writer/critics, students of writing—in short, anyone who studies literature with even a relative degree of seriousness—rather than examining passages of description, rather than scrutinizing dialogue exchanges, rather than diagramming plots, zooms in first on that which in the work is didactic. People who study literature are quick with the pencil to mark any passage which stands out as a declaration of the writer's ideas. We look for what the poet John D. Smith calls, "the quotable line," and when works fail to provide that quotable line, we are disappointed. Richard Kostelanetz's test for a poet's worth: "Can you remember a line from a poem?" Think of your favorite poets, your favorite fiction writers, your favorite dramatists: invariably, you'll be able to quote lines from those writers. We can all quote lines from Shakespeare, Milton, Yeats, Eliot, Melville, Conrad, Poe, Austen, James, Tennyson, Wordsworth, Blake, Wilde, and dozens of other writers. Now think of those lines you have in your head: invariably they will have something in common, and what this is most likely to be is that they are declarative statements, proclamations of truth, lines which, almost without exception, make sweeping generalizations about the condition of man or which make overt recommendations about how man should behave. The lines are *didactic*. Denis Donoghue once during a lecture on Cormac McCarthy's masterpiece, *Blood Meridian*, stopped the lecture and looked up from his book and said, "When I'm reading a book, there are sentences which leap off the page and beg to be underlined, to be noted," and then he read a series of one-liners delivered by the character of Judge Holden, McCarthy's Nietzschean aphoristic sultan. These lines are the lines the writing instructors would have their students excise from their stories and poems, turning their work into un-memorable works which are guaranteed never to be cited or quoted. These lines provide the stuff of debate and discussion. They are the meat of literary criticism. This is why when we read a collection of criticism of a given author's work, we see the same passages cited over and over again. We claim to prefer work that is not didactic, but it is the didactic in art that we cri-tique, that we keep in our minds long after closing our books.

All art is didactic, but not all that is didactic is art.

Only great artists fail.

Jack London is a didactic writer first and foremost. He writes to scream his ideas. He knows the difference between didactic writing and Art, and occasionally writes a story that can be considered Art, if we take one of the primary quali-ties of art to be the production of a problem rather than the solution of a problem. If a problem is solvable, then it's really not much of a problem at all. And so great writers are those who *can't solve problems*, those who create problems *they fail to solve*.

The greatest writers are also the greatest failures. That is because only great writers strive for the ultimately unattain-able Platonic "Ideal."

To succeed, one must merely set one's sights low. Romance writers do not fail. Nor do mystery writers. When what one sets out to do is possible to do, then one may succeed.

William Faulkner judges writers on their "splendid failure to do the impossible," on how well they "failed to match the dream of perfection."

Only great writers fail. Shakespeare wrote the *Henry VI* plays and *Titus Andronicus*. Faulkner wrote *A Fable* and *The*

Reivers. Hemingway's *Islands in the Stream.* At least half of Mailer's books are grand flops. Henry Miller schlogged away at *The Rosy Crucifixion.* Joyce's *Finnegans Wake,* Melville's *Pierre,* Pynchon's *Vineland,* Ben Johnson's *Cataline,* Cormac McCarthy's *Outer Dark,* James's *The Princess Casamassima,* scores of poems by Frost, Yeats, Wordsworth, Coleridge, Ashbery, Dryden, Pope, Dickinson, Tennyson. Great writers fail greatly.

Mediocre writers never fail.

John Hawkes has never failed. Cheever never failed. Joyce Carol Oates never failed, nor Stephen Crane, nor Robert Stone, nor Phillip Roth. Sue Grafton's alphabet-titled mystery series, now popular at the supermarket checkout stands, will never falter. Not because she is great, but because she is mediocre, because the task she sets for herself is easily attainable.

Jack London's failures are magnificent in their wretchedness. *Burning Daylight* would compete admirably for the honor of being one of the worst books ever penned. Some of his short stories—"In the Time of Prince Charley," for instance—are so bad, are so truly rotten, that they are almost parodies of bad writing.

A book can only be a failure truly if it is written by a great author. To fail, a book must disappoint grandly, must abuse our expectations of greatness. Writers of inconsequence do not fail—they merely don't succeed. They merely just don't matter.

Great art is greatly difficult, and the difficulty of great art is moral in nature. Stylistically difficult shenanigans, like those practiced by the L-A-N-G-U-A-G-E poets, do not constitute greatness, even though those shenanigans are difficult indeed. It is moral difficulty which generates the difficulty in great works of art. Moral difficulty is merely another name for didactic difficulty, for all morality is predicated on the implicit recommendation and mandate that other people follow the recommended and/or mandated behavior.

American writers of today, had they been living three hundred years ago, would have been standing on stumps in the town square preaching. They would have been wandering the countryside preaching the word of the Lord. All writers are didacticists and want to tell the world how it should go about the business of living, thinking *their* morals to be the *correct* morals.

The didactic intent in the greatest works of modern, non-religious art may be buried beneath the surface of the text, but it is, nonetheless, there.

Concerning didacticism, London, in his essay "On the Writer's Philosophy of Life," writes:

> Every permanently successful writer has possessed [an ordinary working] philosophy [of life]. It was a view peculiarly his own. It was a yardstick by which he measured all things which came to his notice. By it he focused the characters he drew, the thoughts he uttered. Because of it his work was sane, normal, and fresh. It was something new, something the world wished to hear. It was his, and not a garbled mouthing of things the world had already heard.
>
> But make no mistake. The possession of such a philosophy does not imply a yielding to the didactic impulse. Because one may have pronounced views on any question is no reason that he assault the public ear with a novel with a purpose, and for that matter, no reason that he should not. But it will be noticed, however, that this philosophy of the writer rarely manifests itself in a desire to sway the world to one side or the other of any problem.

It would seem that London believes that didacticism is a negative thing in fiction, that the writer should not be a vehicle for instructing the reader. But in contradistinction to a description of what he considers to be hacks, among whom he places himself in his article "First Aid to Rising Authors," London writes that unlike hacks, who write for "cash" and "belly need," there is the other class of writers: "those who have, or think they have, a message the world needs or would be glad to hear; and those whose lives have been cast on hard ground and in barren places, striving to make the belly need." He says:

> They are the heavenly, fire flashing, fire bringing creatures, so made that they must speak though ears be deaf and the heavens fall. History is full of them, and attests that they have spoken, whether on the graven tablets of Mount Sinai, in the warring pamphlets of a later period, or in the screaming Sunday newspaper of today. Their ambition is to teach, to help to uplift. Self is no determining factor. They were not created primarily for their own good, but for the good of the world. Honor, glory, and power do not attract them. A crust of bread and a beggar's garb meet all their material desires.

These writers, these writers who teach, who help to uplift, who are selfless and create "for the good of the world," would seem to be the great writers in London's mind. And it is obvious that although he does not claim to be one of them, although he actively poses as a man opposed to didacticism of the highest order, he nonetheless is a teaching writer, a writer who would create art over hackwork. In a letter to Cloudesley Johns, London writes:

> Don't you tell the reader the philosophy of the road (except where you are actually there as participant in the first person). Don't you tell the reader. Don't. Don't. Don't. But HAVE YOUR CHARACTERS

TELL IT BY THEIR DEEDS, ACTIONS, TALK, ETC. Then, and not until then, are you writing fiction and not a sociological paper upon a certain sub-stratum of society.

And get the atmosphere. Get the breath and thickness to your stories, and not only the length (which is the mere narration). The reader, since it is fiction, doesn't want your dissertations on the subject, your observations, your knowledge as your knowledge, your thoughts about it, your ideas—BUT PUT ALL THOSE THINGS WHICH ARE YOURS INTO THE STORIES, INTO THE TALES, ELIMINATING YOURSELF (except when in the first person as participant). AND THIS WILL BE THE ATMOSPHERE. AND THIS ATMOSPHERE WILL BE YOU, DON'T YOU UNDERSTAND, YOU! YOU! YOU! And for this, and for this only, will the critics praise you, and the public appreciate you, and your work be art. In short, you will then be the artist; do not do it, and you will be the artisan. . . . Atmosphere stands always for the elimination of the artist, that is to say, the atmosphere is the artist; and when there is no atmosphere and the artist is yet there, it simply means that the machinery is creaking and that the reader hears it.

Eliminate the artist; resist the urge to instruct through instruction; if you are to instruct, do so through atmosphere; know the difference between artist and artisan. Although London here outlines artistic criteria for the short story which resemble James's and Poe's near-definitive statements concerning fictional aesthetics, nonetheless London, even during the period in which this statement is made, quite simply cannot resist the opportunity to conk us over the head with his own philosophies. To wit, the opening of his 1899 short story, "In a Far Country," one of London's earliest tales of the North:

When a man journeys into a far country, he must be prepared to forget many of the things he has learned, and to acquire such customs as are inherent with existence in the new land; he must abandon the old ideals and the old gods, and oftentimes he must reverse the very codes by which his conduct has hitherto been shaped. To those who have the protean faculty of adaptability, the novelty of such change may even be a source of pleasure; but to those who happen to be hardened to the ruts in which they were created, the pressure of the altered environment is unbearable, and they chafe in body and in spirit under the new restrictions which they do not understand. This chafing is bound to act and react, producing divers evils and leading to various misfortunes. It were better for the man who cannot fit himself to the new groove to return to his own country; if he delay too long, he will surely die.

The man who turns his back upon the comforts of an elder civilization, to face the savage youth, the primordial simplicity of the North, may estimate success at an inverse ratio to the quantity and quality of his hopelessly fixed habits.

Here the didactic machinery creaks loud and clear: London has begun his story with a veritable essay concerning Darwinian notions of adaptability, the difference between man in society and man in nature, the role of moral codes with respect to the location in which those codes are relevant. Instead of rendering the dissertation on these subjects in the first-person, as he himself recommends to Cloudesley Johns, London delivers the opening through an omniscient, third-person narrator whose observations assume the attitude of godlike veracity. London tells Johns not to deliver knowledge as knowledge, not to deliver dissertations on the subject, to keep his observations to himself and render them through atmosphere only. But the opening of this story, like so much else in London's fiction, contradicts utterly his own very good advice. The story which follows is a working-out of the thesis which features two rookies to the North who end up wintering together in a cabin in the frozen waste. Neither character has heeded the narrator's opening philosophies and observations, and as a result of their ignorance of what the narrator knows so well, the characters are unable to cope, are unable to adapt, to their new surroundings. They fail to adjust their codes of behavior and social interaction, and they consequently get cabin fever, growing increasingly hostile toward each other until finally Weatherbee plants an axe in Percy Cuthfert's spine and kills him, while at the same time Cuthfert blasts Weatherbee with a pistol. The characters do not understand the code outlined by London's omniscient narrator at the story's onset, and therefore they die. Stripped of the opening few paragraphs, the story would read as a fine work of fiction, one which follows the dictates London outlines to Johns; however, the paragraphs remain, and the story, rather than being a work of pure fiction, is a thesis-story which first presents the thesis, then dramatizes the point with the standard trappings of fiction, then concludes inevitably with dramatic "proof" of the truth of the thesis.

The works we usually consider to be the greatest works of art are those which present moral dilemmas, moral *difficulty*. *Hamlet* interests us more than a Stephen King novel because Hamlet's dilemma is morally ambiguous. *The Scarlet Letter* would not be the great book it is if we were able to easily pronounce judgment on Hester Prynne. There is no way to escape moral intent in a work of art, however, even if the work claims to be "art for art's sake," because art for art's sake itself is a moral stance, a stance which claims that art for art's sake is preferable to supposedly didactic work. The recommendation, the act of preferring, is moral, and the art-product is consequently didactic.

America has a rich tradition of didactic writers of varying degrees of aesthetic quality. We're a nation founded by Calvinist Puritans, after all. Our earliest "American" literature is steeped in religious didacticism. With Milton and Bunyan paving the road of aesthetic principle, our literature has always been one of moralizing, with few authors even in contemporary times straying from the path.

The problem we face aesthetically, given that all art is didactic, is choosing what *kind* of didacticism is meet and good. Why should didacticism which preaches a gospel of art be considered better art than didacticism which preaches a social philosophy? Or which preaches a disagreeable thesis?

London has conflicting notions about the purpose behind his own writing. He can't decide if he is an artist dedicated to pure aesthetics, or a writer of the people, a hard-core naturalist whose mission it is to rip up the streets and show us the flowing sewers beneath. Is Jack London a great artist? This depends on just what we define an "artist" to be. If we judge London's work according to the aesthetics of the rich, then he doesn't cut the mustard. And even if we judge London according to his own standards, we run into trouble: since his own standards shift according to whether he is feeling sympathy for the working man or contempt for him, is he always a great artist? His daughter, Joan London, cites him as saying to a young radical who came to interview him:

> I dream of beautiful horses and fine soil. I dream of
> the beautiful things I own up in Sonoma County. And
> I write for no other purpose than to add to the beauty
> that now belongs to me. I write a book for no other

reason than to add three or four hundred acres to my magnificent estate. I write a story with no other purpose than to buy a stallion. To me, my cattle are far more interesting than my profession.

As reported in Richard O'Connor's biography of London, this is the same man whom Sinclair Lewis is referring to in the following anecdote:

> The "literary high point" of his Carmel experience, Lewis said, was witnessing Jack's glancing, bewildered encounter with the work of Henry James, which to Lewis represented "the clash between Main Street and Beacon Street that is eternal in American culture." He recalled, "At a neighboring cabin Jack picked up James's *The Wings of the Dove* and, standing there, short, burly, in a soft shirt and black tie, the Master read aloud in a bewildered way while Henry James's sliding, slithering, gliding verbiage unwound itself on and on. Jack banged the book down and wailed, 'Do any of you know what all this junk is about?'"

To London, James's work is devoid of what he seeks in art. London claims to seek truth, a moral and factual truth that will endure and, as he says in "What Life Means to Me," help man to achieve what he believes to be "the nobility and excellence of the human." This is the same man who hopes that his work will endure and enrich the lives of his readers by telling the truth about our lives. London writes in his essay "These Bones Shall Rise Again":

> Dealing only with the artist, be it understood, only those artists will go down who have spoken true of us. Their truth must be the deepest and most significant, their voices clear and strong, definite and coherent. Half-truths and partial-truths will not do, nor will

> thin piping voices and quavering lays. There must be
> the cosmic quality in what they sing. They must seize
> upon and press into enduring art-forms the vital facts
> of our existence. They must tell why we have lived, for
> without any reason for living, depend upon it, in the
> time to come, it will be as though we had never lived.

London believes that works which will endure are those which
tap into the vital core of humanity, into the common denominators of the species. His aesthetic philosophy is in keeping
with many other writers of his time, and indeed London's aim
in the above passage resembles Joseph Conrad's aesthetic as
outlined in his "Preface to *The Nigger of the 'Narcissus'*" in
which he writes:

> His [the artist's] appeal is less loud, more profound,
> less distinct, more stirring—and sooner forgotten. Yet
> its effect endures forever. The changing wisdom of
> successive generations discards ideas, questions facts,
> demolishes theories. But the artist appeals to that part
> of our being which is not dependent on wisdom, to
> that in us which is a gift and not an acquisition—and,
> therefore, more permanently enduring.

The striking resemblance between the two writers' aesthetic
notions illustrates, at least, that London's thoughts concerning the aims of the artist align themselves with writers far
greater than he.

London doesn't seem to take his own advice often—certainly no one's machinery creaks and moans louder than his
when he is on a roll, not Norris, Crane, Dreiser, nor even
Harriet Beecher Stowe. All too often he stands on his writerly
soapbox and delivers sermons which do nothing *but* call attention to the artist. London's strong feelings for the working
class from which he hails consistently get entangled with his

attempts to create high art. But although he may be neither a consummate nor a consistent artist, he is a writer whose works endure. And the endurance of an artist's work is as important to London—London the Writer of the People—as the purely aesthetic aspects of the art. In "These Bones Shall Rise Again," London writes, "That man of us who seizes upon the salient facts of our life, who tells what we thought, what we were, and for what we stood—that man shall be the mouthpiece to the centuries, and so long as they listen he shall endure." For millions of people, London has indeed seized upon the salient facts of life—and if not the facts, then the contradictions, which, in the final analysis, just may be the only true facts. His books remain in print, and though not necessarily cherished by academia, remain, if nothing else, the literary cornerstones of the people he most associated himself with—the workers of Oakland. Nothing endures like shame, like poverty, like destitution and the wreckage of humanity.

Wealth comes and goes, but poverty endures.

Jack London makes many high and mighty claims in his life about the function of art and the role of aesthetics in the production of a work of fiction, and were we to read only his critical commentaries, found, for the most part, in his letters to Cloudesley Johns and occasionally in his autobiographical novels, *Martin Eden*, *John Barleycorn*, and *The Road*, we would expect to find fiction which resembles that of Chekhov, James, or Poe among London's work. Certainly, when London is at his best—in such stories as "The White Silence," "The Son of the Wolf," "Where the Trail Forks," "The Law of Life," "The Devil's Dice-Box," "To the Man on Trail," "In a Far Country," "To Build a Fire," "Odyssey of the North," and "Love of Life"—his work is without question fine indeed, rich with ambiguity and depth of understanding of the human condition, the prose careful and clean and relatively free of the pseudo-philosophy we find clogging the pages of his weaker work. But in most of London's fiction, he is guilty of a thorough and deliberate didacticism which not only intrudes on the artistry of the work, but often actually overwhelms it, so that, in the final analysis, the tales more resemble fiction-alized essays than works of what we would customarily call "fiction."

Jack London is what I call a Thesis Writer, and we find the seeds of this condition in his earliest attempts at writing fiction, the handful of stories written before the publication of his first book. The thesis writer is not an uncommon character in the history of American literature: Stephen Crane is a thesis writer of the lowest order, his stories dramatized enactments of social commentaries he felt compelled to make ("The Open Boat"—nature doesn't care, "Maggie"—we are products of our environment, et cetera); Dos Passos is often a thesis writer, and the *USA* trilogy is perhaps the longest-winded diatribe on capitalism posing as fiction ever written; Upton Sinclair, Steinbeck, Pearl S. Buck, Sinclair Lewis—all to greater and lesser degrees have their respective axes to grind, and when the sparks fly, there is no question that the axe is intended to be used on our notions of the way the world works and what we should do to alter its condition. Such contemporary writers as Alice Walker, Richard Ford, Robert Olen Butler, and T. C. Boyle suffer the same lamentable and tedious malady, unable to resist blasting their weak and sophomoric social philosophies and squandering what little talent they have on the assumption that they are sociologists whose observations are jackhammered into the monolith of literary and political history. Missing from thesis writers are the complexities of thought which make fiction endure the ages, for if a story can be reduced to a simple thesis, then once that thesis is elucidated, the story is a mystery solved.

Great works of fiction invite not only multiple readings, but multiple interpretations. As time passes, the works, because of their multiple layers of meaning, change, evolve, mutate. A story which is based on a thesis, however, remains forever static, cast in the mold it has forged for itself.

In James McClintock's *Jack London's Strong Truths*, he writes that, in many of London's artistically inferior works, he employs "an essay-exemplum type of construction reminiscent of earlier writers who prefixed rambling sermons to their stories." McClintock argues that this type of setup is inferior and makes for rotten fiction. He notes:

> In the essay-exemplum stories the narrator was constrained to speak in what can only be the author's authoritative voice rather than through a *persona*. Most of the explicit comments made by the narrator are awkwardly overbearing and dogmatic in their attempts to force ideas upon the reader and commit the story-teller to arriving at definite conclusions.

It is these definite conclusions which, by definition, make the stories solvable, and therefore likely to be buried by a literary history which prefers ambiguity. *The Scarlet Letter* and *Moby Dick* will be new to each new generation of readers, whereas didactic fiction will fade into oblivion.

The problem with identifying an author's greatness is the implicit presence of a cogent system of aesthetic standards by which to judge the author's merit. It seems to me that this problem, an issue for philosophers and writers from Aristotle to Kant, Plato to Gass, has never found a satisfactory solution; but though we have as yet (nor will ever have, hopefully) no clear-cut objective criteria with which to judge the relative merit of works of art, we find some common denominators. Great art has been variously said both to please and to instruct. This leads us to the problems of defining "pleasing" and "instructing." Generally, pleasing entails appealing to both a sense of "truth" and an appeal to the higher faculties of the mind, as Walter Pater writes, in his "Conclusion" to *The Renaissance*, "proposing frankly to give nothing but the highest quality to your moments as they pass, and simply for those moments' sake." Pleasing, then, is achieved outside of morality, within the perceptive, sensual mind; pleasure achieved through the experience of art occurs outside the context of social proprieties. Oscar Wilde writes, in his preface to *The Picture of Dorian Gray*, "There is no such thing as a moral or an immoral book," and this statement echoes Pater's: art is for pleasure. The idea of art for art's sake, a recurrent rebel yell in answer to overtly didactic art, is quite impossible, however, to put into practice.

All art is informed by didactic intent. The very notion of beauty is involved with morality, if we consider beauty something to aspire to. Behind every artistic act is a moralizing artist. Oscar Wilde spent a great deal of energy promoting his notion of art for art's sake, and the act of promotion itself was a didactic act: the choice to teach, to recommend, is a moral choice, as are, I believe, all human choices. Wilde's art is nothing if not instructive, preaching a mode of living based on his notion of aesthetics. We can not escape moral intention in an artistic act, and this is, quite simply, because we are moral creatures. Art is not created, nor does it consequently exist, merely to be observed: art is always didactic.

This is not to say all that is didactic is Art. Some of London's very worst work oozes and drips with his didactic intent. His novel *Before Adam*, a journey into the dreams of a protagonist who nightly goes back to his caveman former self, smells so heavily of Darwin that the novel is almost comic.

Donald Barthelme writes, in his essay "Not-Knowing," "Art is not difficult because it wishes to be difficult, but because it wishes to be art." If Barthelme is right, then the "easy" art of London, for instance in *Before Adam*, fails. It is not art, because it is not difficult. And this is usually the case when the didactic intent of a work of art overpowers the aesthetic function of art. If all art is inherently didactic, then to lard a work, already didactic by nature, with didacticism, is to destroy whatever artistic merit the work might have.

This is why the works of Upton Sinclair, Harriet Beecher Stowe, and so forth, have faded in importance while works of writers whose work is not overtly didactic remains vital. Polemic may indeed attain the condition of art, but only if the issue involved in the polemic is a timeless issue and not a topical one. *Candide* and *Gulliver's Travels* are both largely polemical works, but both balance pleasure and instruction, both deal generally with timeless issues, both resist the temptation, ever present for an artist, to see only the present and the specific. When a specific issue becomes irrelevant, so does the art spawned by the issue. Witness the fade to black Dos Passos has suffered.

Even when we're not moralizing and preaching from our soapboxes, we're preaching that we shouldn't be preaching. From Bradford, Taylor, and Bradstreet, to Pynchon, Gaddis, and Cormac McCarthy, we've been telling people how to live—what to think, what to do, what to believe, what to love, and what to hate. When God died in the 19th century, we started preaching even more zealously, clawing at the heavens and in the dirt looking for answers to what might prove a meaningless existence. Our popular literature and film always boils down to a rehashing of typical Western-culture mythologies which mirror the fairy tales of the Bible: the good guys fight the bad guys, and the good guys beat and punish the bad guys. In the literature of the past 150 years, the masters—Hawthorne, Melville, Faulkner, Hemingway—have this in common: they ask the question, Just who are the good guys, and who are the bad guys? What *is* good, and what *is* evil? However, they still preach: they just muddy the waters as thoroughly as possible, never arguing that we stray from what is "right," but, instead, arguing that we need to reassess just what *is* indeed right. It's still preaching.

If this muddying of the waters while preaching moral standards is one of the qualities we find in what we consider great literature (and it seems to me that it is), then we should find London muddying his waters like the other greats. Jack London has a weighty body of work which most certainly preaches absolutes in terms of just what constitutes good and what constitutes evil; note *The People of the Abyss*, *The Iron Heel*, *Revolution and Other Essays*, *The War of the Classes*, and so forth. Nonetheless, he has a great body of work that is richly ambiguous in terms of the lessons it preaches, works that compare favorably with the best of Hawthorne and Melville, the masters of American ambiguity.

Assessing an artist's relative greatness becomes increasingly difficult in proportion to the degree to which the author is overtly didactic.

X

LONDON'S FICTION:
THE CONFLICT AND ITS RESOLUTION

Jack London's fiction breaks down into three distinct types, reflecting the thesis, antithesis, and synthesis of the ideas that resulted from his upbringing in the working-class ghettos of Oakland. Frederick Feied, in his book *No Pie in the Sky: the Hobo as American Cultural Hero in the Works of Jack London, John Dos Passos, and Jack Kerouac*, writes that London's

> thesis was always the struggle for individual supremacy or biological survival—the supreme law, whether of the jungle or the frozen Alaska wastes, according to Nietzsche and Darwin. And the anti-thesis, often developed just as forcefully within the same story, as in the case of *Martin Eden* and *The Sea Wolf*, consisted of attacks on Nietzschean philosophy or an indictment of individualism. . . .

The way Feied treats London is as a writer who feels two opposing forces tugging at his sleeves: one force would free the workers from the chains of capitalist oppression and would create a utopian workers' state à la Marx; the other is a naturalist force that recognizes only power, will, and nature as the determinant elements of life, à la Nietzsche and Darwin.

Feied does not find that London ever resolves these conflicts. London is either the writer of the collection *The Strength of the Strong*, which contains London's finest Socialist stories, among them the masterful "South of the Slot," or he is the writer of the Northland tales who creates *The Son of the Wolf*, which includes some of London's best Darwinian/Nietzschean tales, such as "To the Man on Trail," "The White Silence," "The Devil's Dice-Box," "An Odyssey of the North," and "In a Far Country." London's better stories contain elements of both philosophies—are both Socialistic and Nietzschean, despite his attempts to make the stories overtly of one camp or the other. His weaker works, such as the ridiculous Socialist story, "The Strength of the Strong" or the philosophically ugly and overtly racist Nietzschean story "The Son of the Wolf," make their respective cases unequivocally and relentlessly. London's theses come through without ambiguity, and although he probably considered the stories successes (he did, after all, title the collections after the worst stories in the collections), the only real success of the stories was their clarity of intention.

At his worst, London is a thesis writer.

When London is at his best, he is a thesis writer who fails to communicate his thesis. This is why, when attacked for presenting Wolf Larsen as a raving bully in *The Sea Wolf*,[1] London has to explain to the public and the critics that *The Sea Wolf* is an attack on individualism, not a work in praise of it. His failure to communicate his "thesis" results in one of his finest works of Art.

As does his failure in his other great works.

"The Strength of the Strong" presents a clear thesis: Capitalism is evil, and Socialism will eventually dominate societal structures. The story is set in prehistoric times, and the characters are apelike men with protruding jaws and hairy backs, characters with names like "Pig-Jaw," "Long Beard," and

"Big-Fat," this last being the story's caveman/capitalist villain, named for the fat cats we find caricatured in the Socialist cartoons of the turn of the century, little fat-boys like the mustachioed top-hatted mogul of Monopoly board-game fame. Big-Fat gathers land, capital, and self-issued money—he even invents booze with the express purpose of keeping his proles foamy, bleary-eyed, weak, and enslaved by addiction—and tyrannizes the "Fish Eaters," keeping them distracted from their enslavement to the capitalistic system he has created by periodically declaring war against the neighboring tribe, the "Meat Eaters." The servile work beasts under Big-Fat's rule eventually get fed up, overthrow him, and set up a Socialist society, and they live happily ever after, chomping away at the campfire on the barbecued entrails of animals they've killed with their own bare hands, reaping the profits of their own toil. The story is as ridiculous as a story can be and has nowhere near the punch of London's actual Socialist essays in which he avoids cavemen, deals with real human beings and real incidents from life, and writes with such verve and passion as to incite fear in the literary and social establishments of his day. The story's narrator, Long Beard, concludes:

> Some day . . . all the fools will be dead and then all live men will go forward. The strength of the strong will be theirs, and they will add their strength together, so that, of all the men in the world, not one will fight with another. There will be no guards nor watchers on the walls. . . . And all men will be brothers, and no man will lie idle in the sun and be fed by his fellows. And all that will come to pass in the time when the fools are dead. . . .

The generalizations fall flat and sound like watered-down Socialist propaganda. London's speeches and essays pack more punch than this story's fade-out end.

London can be equally silly on the side of Nietzschean superiority and Darwinistic inevitability. "The Son of the Wolf," for example, is really not much more than a tract on Anglo-Saxon superiority, chock full of debased and bastardized Nietzschean aphorisms. Scruff Mackenzie, the Blond Beast of the story, is a lonely prospector who finds his gonads tingling in need of a wife, and so he troops on over to an Eskimo encampment famed for its good-looking nookie. He proceeds to outgift all the Eskimo warriors, resultant of his White backwoods prowess of turning resources into commodities, and gets the blessing of the Chief for the hand of his hottie daughter. The local boys, however, are not pleased, not at all. Scruff gives them some speeches concerning the terrors of their position should they decide to mess with him. For instance, he says,

> Now will I tell you of my people, who are the mightiest
> of all the peoples, who rule in all the lands. At first we
> hunt as I hunt, alone. After that we hunt in packs; and
> at last, like the cariboo-run, we sweep across all the
> land. Those whom we take into our lodges live; those
> who will not come die. . . . Listen to the Law of the
> Wolf: Whoso taketh the life of one Wolf, the forfeit
> shall ten of his people pay. In many lands has the price
> been paid; in many lands shall it yet be paid.

Scruff is the tough-guy Anglo-Saxon, the colonialist warrior who will bring down his superior culture on them, who is the representative of the finest of the finest of humanity. He is Nietzsche's Übermensch, the lone superior warrior.

The Darwin string is plucked in this story as well. Describing Mackenzie's fistfight with one of the Eskimos, London writes:

> At first he felt compassion for his enemy; but this fled
> before the primal instinct of life, which in turn gave

way to the lust of slaughter. The ten thousand years
of culture fell from him, and he was a cave-dweller,
doing battle for his female.

Primal instincts, cave-dwellers, duking it out for "his female"— Scruff has reverted to his roots, his Darwinistic genes
bubbling and foaming up in a retrogressive atavistic soup of
hormones. Unless one is offended by the story, it's hard not to
laugh at it. Scruff, of course, whips the asses of all the lesser-
developed Eskimos, gets the girl, and shows the "primitives"
who's boss, Anglo-Saxon-style. Scruff Mackenzie is not only
more civilized, but he can out-savage the savage.

These stories in which London succeeds at conveying his
thesis are the kinds his detractors point at when they're belit-
tling his genius. Unfortunately for London, he published them
and scores more of similar ilk. But he was a writer working
for a living, and they sold, and so simple economics dictated
the necessity for their publication. London is not always such
a success, however. He often fails to communicate his theses;
he often writes stories in which he just can't quite get it right,
in which his lines of demarcation grow a bit hazy, in which he
fails so well that he creates works of Art.

London's most successful Socialist story is "South of the
Slot." The story's title refers to the trolley rails that run the
length of Market Street in San Francisco. The rails divide
the town: North of the rails reside the wealthy, the business-
men, the flashy cash of swaggering San Francisco. To this
day, North of Market is the financial district, the famous
skyline of the city. South of the rails, South of Market, South
of "the Slot," is where the laborers live. Today the area South
of Market is largely either active warehouses or warehouses
converted into loft space. It is being yuppified, as are all
beaten neighborhoods colonized by artists, but in London's

time the area was a mixture of factories, warehouses, and
ramshackle homes for the workers employed in the factories,
warehouses, and shipyards of South San Francisco. It was the
workers' ghetto, where could be found "the factories, slums,
laundries, machine-shops, boiler works, and the abodes of the
working class." London features the same neighborhood in
a silly Socialist fantasy called "The Dream of Debs," which
begins with the premise of a glorious general strike. In this
story, the workers bring anarchy by refusing to work and
eventually bring the capitalists to their knees, quite literally,
begging at the doorsteps of the workers. The area "South of
the Slot" serves as a metaphor for what we call "the other side
of the tracks": it is Queens, it is South Chicago, it is Watts, it
is Oakland, it is the neighborhood in which the workers who
produce the capital live. London writes, "The Slot was the
metaphor that expressed the class cleavage of Society, and no
man crossed this metaphor, back and forth, more successfully
than Freddie Drummond."

Freddie Drummond is a sociology professor at the University
of California, and he writes anti-labor books, which are hailed
as masterworks by the captains of industry for their exposure
of the sloth and stupidity of the workers, for their endorsement
of the status quo. Drummond's book *The Unskilled Laborer* is

> hailed everywhere as an able contribution to the litera-
> ture of progress, and as a splendid reply to the literature
> of discontent. Politically and economically it was noth-
> ing if not orthodox. Presidents of great railway systems
> bought whole editions of it to give to their employees.

To gather materials for his anti-labor books, Drummond de-
scends into the working-class neighborhood "South of the
Slot" and lives and works with the laborers—much as London
did himself in order to write *The People of the Abyss.*

Robert Louis Stevenson was one of London's favorite writers, and following along the lines of Stevenson's doppelgänger novel, *Dr. Jeckyl and Mr. Hyde*, London splits Drummond into two personalities—Freddie Drummond, the mild-mannered, conservative, proper, middle-class scholar who obeys all forms and rules and proprieties, nicknamed "Cold Storage" by his colleagues at the university; and "Big" Bill Totts, the persona Drummond assumes when he's slumming with the workers, researching for his next attack on them.

Bill Totts becomes everything Freddie "Cold Storage" Drummond is not. He works with his hands; he joins the union; he carries himself upright and firmly; he is hearty, loud, quick with his fists, loyal to the workers, a roustabout and drinker and no stranger to women: "Freddie Drummond did not care for dancing . . . Bill Totts never missed the nights at the various dancing clubs." He is a man who, unlike the socially crafted Drummond, follows his instincts. London writes:

> From doing the thing for the need's sake, he came to doing the thing for the thing's sake. He found himself regretting as the time drew near for him to go back to his lecture-room and his inhibition. And he often found himself waiting with anticipation for the dreamy time to pass when he could cross the Slot and cut loose and play the devil.

Drummond becomes two people in the story and increasingly finds them at odds: the one a union-busting, condescending, tight-assed professor; the other "thoroughly a workman, a genuine denizen of South of the Slot . . . as class-conscious as the average of his kind . . . his hatred for a scab even exceeded that of the average loyal union man."

In the professorial world, Drummond eventually decides to marry—appropriately, of course—the daughter of the head of the Philosophy Department of the university. His fiancée, Catherine Van Vorst, is as cold and reserved as he, and "possesse[s] an inhibition equal to Drummond's." In the work-beast world South of the Slot, Bill Totts falls for a union-organizing woman named Mary Condon.

The story's climax is a blaze of frenzy.[2] The workers of San Francisco have called a strike—a meat strike—and Drummond, seated in a carriage next to Catherine, gets caught between the billy-clubbing cops and hired thugs of the businesses on one side and the workers who are trying to block the scabs' access to the hotels to which the police-escorted scabs are trying to deliver meat. The battle scene is graphic and bloody, a maelstrom of broken skulls and cracked bones and wonderfully paced violence. In the midst of the fight sits Drummond, a man with deep-rooted sympathies for both sides.

So well does London present both sides of Drummond's dual life that neither character is despicable: both characters are good men who, in their respective communities are productive, respected, and in roles of leadership. So when the riot begins, we wait for Drummond to make his decision. Either choice is a bad one, for neither side is wholly in the right or in the wrong. Drummond, watching the working men be beaten by the legal and authorized clubs of the police, "emit[s] an unearthly and uncultured yell and [rises] to his feet," and then he joins the riot and helps the workers to escape down Third Street, back South of the Slot, where Drummond spends the rest of his days as the labor leader William Totts.

Because the story keeps its didactic intent fairly in check, London succeeds. He refrains from passing judgment on the wealthy, and he doesn't romanticize the working poor. Rather, he presents a realistic scene, based on the actual San Francisco labor riots of 1901, from the viewpoint of an objective,

third-person narrator. When Drummond makes the choice
to become and remain William Totts, we're not necessarily
cheering for him; we do, however, understand his position.
London has held back, chosen to stand on the ground rather
than on a soapbox, and the Socialist message of the piece
is well buried beneath the truly memorable and believable
story—Socialism isn't even mentioned in the story. It's not
necessarily a masterpiece of fiction in terms of classical and
contemporary aesthetic criteria, but it's no slouch either.

One of London's most successful Darwinistic/Nietzs-
chean stories is "To the Man on Trail." The central character
is London's Northland Wise Man, the Malemute Kid. The
Malemute Kid is an upgrade of London's early Wise Man, the
Frisco Kid, featured in two of London's earliest works of fiction. The Frisco Kid is a tramp who makes do in the city and
who is a type we all know: the bum savant. London presents
the Frisco Kid as an example of counter-culture intelligence,
an example of life on the fringe of citified social structures.
The Malemute Kid, on the other hand, is a more highly developed creature, and is no tramp. The tramp, according to
London,

> is one of two kinds of men: he is either a discouraged
> worker or a discouraged criminal. Now a discouraged
> criminal, on investigation, proves to be a discouraged
> worker, or the descendant of discouraged workers; so
> that, in the last analysis, the tramp is a discouraged
> worker.[3]

The Frisco Kid is a discouraged worker, but the Malemute
Kid, though most likely a former discouraged worker, is now,
by virtue of his residence in the last frontier, the Northland,
a self-governing man. He becomes for London a kind of
Nietzschean Superman, a sourdough prospector living in the

Yukon and providing a moral center and narrative balance to London's first two collections of short stories.

"To the Man on Trail" is a rewrite of London's story/sketch "A Klondike Christmas." In it, a group of characters, most of them recurring ones in the Northland stories, have gathered at the cabin of the Malemute Kid to have a Christmas dinner and get hammered on the Malemute Kid's special booze. The story opens,

> "Dump it in."
> "But I say, Kid, isn't that going it a little too strong? Whiskey and alcohol's bad enough; but when it comes to brandy and peppersauce and"—
> "Dump it in. Who's making this punch anyway?" And Malemute Kid smiled benignantly through the clouds of steam. "By the time you've been in this country as long as I have, my son, and lived on rabbit-tracks and salmon-belly, you'll learn that Christmas comes only once per annum. And a Christmas without punch is sinking a hole to bedrock with nary a pay-streak."

Thus far, London has established a number of things. We see that clearly Malemute Kid is the master-of-ceremonies. He is the one who has been in the Northland the longest, and he is the one setting the physical and moral tone of the day. The mixer of the drinks is wary of the potent concoction, but the Kid assures him that a "Christmas without punch" is nary a Christmas at all. So even though they're outside of society, even though they can basically set their own rules, still the Kid recommends some acknowledgment of the forms of society, albeit those forms are slightly amplified, or higher proof, if you will.

When the feast is ready and after a few rounds of song and drink, Malemute Kid raises a toast: "A health to the man on trail this night; may his grub hold out; may his dogs keep their legs; may his matches never miss fire." The toast, innocuous enough in the context of the story, serves as a moral imperative in the story. The man on trail is the man to be respected, the man slugging it through the snow in the darkness of an expansive and barren waste. After the toast, a Northland Santa Claus pulls up outside the cabin:

> Crack! Crack!—they heard the familiar music of the dogwhip, the whining howl of the Malemutes, and the crunch of a sled as it drew up to the cabin. Conversation languished while they waited the issue.

Instead of reindeer, we get sled dogs; instead of sleigh bells, the cracking of a whip; instead of childish glee at the visitor's arrival, we get silent apprehension. And instead of Santa Claus, we get Jack Westondale, who

> seemed, of a verity, the Frost King, just stepped in out of the night. Clasped outside his mackinaw jacket, a beaded belt held two large Colt's revolvers and a hunting knife, while he carried, in addition to the inevitable dogwhip, a smokeless rifle of the largest bore and latest pattern.

Westondale is the Anti-Santa Claus: he brings not gifts, but guns—the possibility of death. He is ostensibly chasing three men who have stolen his team of dogs and who have a two day jump on him, and in pursuit he has dog-mushed seventy-five miles of trail in twelve hours, twice the usual dog-mush rate.

The Malemute Kid scrutinizes Westondale and "attentively studied his face. Nor was he long in deciding that it was fair, honest, and open, and that he liked it." It's not someone's title, not their résumé, not their family name or the company they work for that makes someone trustworthy to the Malemute Kid: it's his face. The men talk, the festivities die down, and Westondale goes to sleep for a few hours to rest up for the chase. When the Malemute Kid is helping Westondale ready his dog team and supplies, the Kid tips his hand: he loads Westondale up with more provisions than he would seem to need, and he tells Westondale of the conditions of the route—not to find the three men and dog team, but into the wilderness. Westondale asks the Malemute Kid,

> "How did you know it? Surely the news can't be ahead of me already?"
>
> "I don't know it; and what's more, I don't want to know it. But you never owned that team you're chasing. Sitka Charley sold it to them last spring. But he sized you up to me as square once, and I believe him. I've seen your face; I like it. And I've seen—why, damn you, hit the high places for salt water and that wife of yours, and,"—Here the Kid unmittened and jerked out his sack.

What we haven't yet found out is what Westondale is running from. We find out directly after he hits the trail. Just fifteen minutes behind Westondale is another Christmas Santa—this one announced with "a jingle of bells" and wearing the red uniform of "a mounted policeman of the Northwest Territory." He is the Law—the representative of civilization and the governing body of the land.

The Mountie tells the men that Westondale has robbed a gaming house and stolen forty thousand dollars. The Malemute Kid, with a glance, keeps the men from giving the mountie information, and finally the Mountie resorts to asking Father Roubeau, who can't lie. The Father gives the information, and the Mountie demands fresh dogs and provisions of the men: "'I'll sign a check on Captain Constantine for five thousand,—here's my papers,—I'm authorized to draw at my own discretion,'" says the Mountie, but the men won't have any of it. He then threatens them with the law: "'Then I'll requisition them in the name of the Queen.'"

This, of course, is the wrong thing to do in the Northland, a couple of thousand miles from the nearest civilization. For in the Northland, though there may be law, the law which is supreme is not the law of "civilization," but of the inhabitants of the land. The Kid, in response to the Mountie's "requisition" smiles "incredulously, [and] glance[s] at his well-stocked arsenal, and the Englishman, realizing his impotency, turn[s] for the door." Justice is not decided by distant governing bodies, but by those people who inhabit the land.

After the Mountie leaves, the men ask the Kid why he wouldn't help the Mountie catch the thief, and the Kid explains that Westondale had entrusted his money—exactly forty thousand dollars—to his partner, who had gambled away the money at the casino from which Westondale stole the money:

> "You'll notice he took exactly what his partner lost,—forty thousand. Well, he's gone out; and what are you going to do about it?"
>
> The Kid glanced round the circle of his judges, noted the softening of their faces, then raised his mug aloft. "So a health to the man on trail this night; may his grub hold out; may his dogs keep their legs; may his matches never miss fire. God prosper him; good luck go with him; and"—
>
> "Confusion to the Mounted Police!" cried Bettles, to the crash of the empty mugs.

The morals are twisted in terms of the codes of civilization, but justice has been served, frontier-style. The police are the villains, for they are not letting justice be served in terms of the men who inhabit the land. But we still question whether or not justice has truly been served.

The Malemute Kid is a Nietzschean character, but he's no Wolf Larsen. He's not killing people and ruling over his little society like a dictator. Instead, he's inventing a moral code that has its foundations in his notions of justice, not merely in strength. The story is a wonderful application of London's ideas of social structures and of justice, and although the story still preaches the lesson of life outside the common realm of society, its preaching is subtle and even a bit ambiguous. At the very least the story is rendered without narrative intrusion. We accept the character of the Malemute Kid because we know him—we've met him on construction sites, in diners, at train stations, on the streets. London shows us that there are alternatives to what we've come to know as the law. What is moral and what is not moral are not necessarily defined by the rules in the books.

Both "South of the Slot" and "To the Man on Trail" have theses, but they are secondary to the tales being told and the characters involved in the tales. When we compare them to such stories as "The Strength of the Strong" and "The Son of the Wolf," it's easy to see that they are superior "thesis" stories. They are fine stories on their own as well and hold up against much of what is currently canonized in academia. "To the Man on Trail" compares favorably both aesthetically and ideologically to such works as Joyce's "Araby," Flannery O'Connor's "A Good Man Is Hard to Find," and Faulkner's "A Rose for Emily," all three of which have their respective stumps from which we are delivered messages.

In London's best stories, however, he still hasn't fused his contradictory ideas; they still either tilt toward Socialism or Fascism, and the reader still finds himself the target of a preacher. It is in *The Call of the Wild* that we find that fusion.

It is to the land that London turns in *The Call of the Wild* because only in a primal land inhabited by primal creatures can London reconcile his contradictory social philosophies. Only if man is an animal and not a moral, and therefore responsible, being can a monetarily successful Socialist find resolution, consolation, and justification for his worldly success and for the failures of those who have not achieved similar success.

In order to create human beings outside of moral systems, London writes such works as *Before Adam*, a ludicrous book along the lines of "The Strength of the Strong." *Before Adam*, in a way, is London's response to John Burroughs' belief that "man is the only animal capable of reasoning." London believes that "We who are so very human are very animal." Defending accusations that he is merely an "animal writer," London writes in "The Other Animals":

> You must not deny your relatives, the other animals. Their history is your history, and if you kick them to the bottom of the abyss, to the bottom of the abyss you go yourself. By them you stand or fall. What you repudiate in them you repudiate in yourself—a pretty spectacle, truly, of an exalted animal striving to disown the stuff of life out of which it is made, striving by use of the very reason that was developed by evolution to deny the processes of evolution that developed it.

That London's greatest books, *The Call of the Wild* and *White Fang*, feature as main characters animals rather than human beings should come as no surprise. It is only in the primitive beast that London can find solace, because the primitive beast is outside morality—in Nietzsche's terms, beyond good and evil. This is why *The Call of the Wild*, his greatest work, is such a success: Buck has no moral quandaries about killing—he is beyond morality. He is what London, or any other human being with a moral system, can never truly be—free.

Before Adam (before man had tasted the fruit of the Tree of the Knowledge of Good and Evil), a decidedly and objectively horrid book, is London's attempt, a failure, at creating a human Buck. His characters, pre-human, are recollected in a dream, and feature names reminiscent of the those in "The Strength of the Strong": Red-Eye, Big-Tooth, Swift One, Broken-Tooth, Lop-Ear, and so forth. (He called his own wife, Charmian, "Mate-Woman.") Bearing witness to the lassitude and lethargy of the Socialist movement around him, London attempts to develop a philosophy with which he can find peace. Of course, the Socialist movement was not pleased with his transition. When London resigned from the Socialist Party, the party replied with anger and contempt, believing that London had betrayed the party because of the greed they saw as a consequence of his success as a money-making writer; the party assured London and its readers that their struggle would, in the end, prevail.[4] History, of course, has proven them thus far erroneous, and London anticipated the Socialist cause's failure. Attempting to develop a workable social philosophy, London decided that, if we view humanity as evolved animals rather than as creatures separated from animals by reason, we would discover reasons for our respective situations. His view resembles Swift's in *Gulliver's Travels*, the Houyhnhnm Master observing that human beings are

> a sort of animals to whose share . . . some small pittance of reason had fallen, whereof [they] made no other use than by its assistance to aggravate [their] natural corruptions, and to acquire new ones which Nature had not given [them].

The Houyhnhnm Master notes that "although he hated the yahoos of this country, yet he no more blamed them for their odious qualities, than he did a *gnnayh* (a bird of prey) for its cruelty, or a sharp stone for cutting his hoof." Gulliver, disgusted with humanity and broken down by the moral contradictions of the human condition, chooses to live out his life in a barn with horses. London knows we are not as guiltless as "*gnnayhs*," and so, like Swift writing about talking horses and yahoos, he finds his refuge writing about pre-human creatures in *Before Adam* and non-human creatures in *The Call of the Wild*. At the end of *Before Adam*, London's narrator says Big-Tooth "is my other-self, and not my real self, but who is so real to me that often I am unable to tell what age I am living in." This unfortunately ridiculous narrator can be both a modern human being and a primordial beast, weaving in and out of moral and animal constructs according to his sleep-cycles. He continues:

> I often wonder about this line of descent. I, the modern, am incontestably a man; yet I, Big-Tooth, the primitive, am not a man. Somewhere, and by straight line of descent, these two parties to my dual personality were connected. . . . One thing only is certain, and that is that Big-Tooth did stamp into the cerebral constitution of one of his progeny all the impressions of his life, and stamped them in so indelibly that the hosts of intervening generations have failed to obliterate them.

When dealing with human beings, only through a fantasy of atavism can London reconcile his philosophies. Man must feel the burden of social responsibility; beast need not. "Wouldn't it be nice if we could be both man and beast?" the book seems to say. At the end of his novel *The Star Rover*, London writes:

> Training is the only moral difference between the man of today and the man of ten thousand years ago. Under

> his thin skin of morality which he has polished on to
> him, he is the same savage that he was ten thousand
> years ago.

If this were true, then we would have no need of Socialism, a political system based on decidedly moral premises. And for London, a belief in both Socialism and in social Darwinism, his crucial contradiction, cannot find its reconciliation in human characters, however desperately he attempts to achieve such a reconciliation.

In *The Call of the Wild*, Buck becomes an atavistic symbol, a substitute for Big-Tooth. Buck, the dog, can exist, whereas missing-links Red-Eye and Big-Tooth cannot. London craved moral freedom, and the preposterous *Before Adam* seems to be a manifestation of that craving. But at the same time, London believed in tenets of Socialism, a system based on moral assumptions. Jacqueline Tavernier-Courbin, on the other hand, writes that London's contradictions "can hardly be seen as a sign of philosophical confusion, but should rather be considered as an example of his wide powers of identification." In his life, London could not reconcile his diametrically opposed feelings toward the common man, and in his works about people, he failed as well. The success of *The Call of the Wild* is that in this book London seems to have achieved the creation of an atavistic being, an ideal creature that lives within a cosmos devoid of morality—The Northland wilderness.

The Call of the Wild is Jack London's least overtly didactic and, consequently, finest longer work of fiction. Imagine a human character similar to Buck the dog, and the work opens itself up to didacticism in the extreme. But Buck is a dog, beyond the moral imperatives of human society. When Buck learns to steal, we do not see it as a didactic commentary on humanity, on poor, oppressed, or disempowered people being reduced to theft; when the man with the club beats Buck into submission, we do not necessarily see the man with the club as a symbol for a cigar-smoking capitalist; when Buck fights with Spitz for leadership of the dog team, we do not read it as a commentary on the brutal and animalistic nature of ascension to power in the field of manual labor; when Buck reverts to the wild, copulates and populates, we don't instantly see the machinery of a Nietzschean writer symbolically announcing the arrival of a race of Supermen in the form of Superdogs. Buck, after all, is a dog, and his doglike actions are in keeping with our perceptions about the beasts. Earle Labor writes, in his essay "Jack London's *Mondo Cane*: "Bâtard," *The Call of the Wild*, and *White Fang*":

> By using canine rather than human protagonists, London was able to say more about [the human] situation than he might have been otherwise permitted by the editors of magazines . . . who were extremely careful not to offend the genteel sensibilities of their Victorian readership.

However, London's aim, it seems to me, is not merely to escape editorial or public censure. *Martin Eden* and *John Barleycorn*, not to mention his public stump speeches and volumes of inflammatory essays, indicate that London doesn't give a hoot about the dainty sensibilities of the "Victorian readership." London, by all accounts, reveled in offending people's sensibilities. Had he wished to tell the tale of a human being regressing, he would have done so, as he did in *Before Adam*. Although Mr. Labor is a London specialist, here he misses the mark.

Buck is an unattainable wish-fantasy for London, his compromise between hatred for the rich and hatred for the poor: if man could only be an animal truly, then the tribulations of class distinctions would vanish into the primordial mire from whence they arose. In his essay Labor argues the obvious—that London's dog-stories are allegories—but he concludes that they are allegories that merely serve the function of creating a "Myth of the Hero"; the rest of his treatment of *The Call of the Wild* quite capably outlines the Myth of the Hero. The idea of Buck-as-Hero is problematic, however. Mythological heroes generally exhibit, in amplified form, the moral values of a given society. Different cultures have different types of heroes, from Odysseus and his combination of honor, guile, strength, and beauty, to Clint Eastwood's portrayals of nameless tough-guy wanderers in the Wild West. Clint Eastwood's no-name, duster-wearing heroes do not epitomize the hero of a Buddhist nation. What Mr. Labor is implying, by saying that Buck serves the function of creating a "Myth of the Hero," is that Buck is indeed a hero. This in turn implies that the popularity of the book is a result of mankind secretly wishing to be thieves, killers, and power-hungry Nietzschean beasts.

Buck is no hero. Neither is he human. He is something else, and that something is a creation wholly and personally Jack London's. Buck is London's fantasy answer to his personal societal moral dilemma. The idea of Buck being a hero in a Judeo-Christian culture just doesn't wash. Mr. Labor seems to be saying that we'd rather be dogs.

The following passage from *The Call of the Wild* Labor claims "is a thematic epitome of the whole work":

> There is an ecstasy that marks the summit of life, and beyond which life cannot rise. And such is the paradox of living, this ecstasy comes when one is most alive, and it comes as a complete forgetfulness that one is alive. This ecstasy, this forgetfulness of living, comes to the artist, caught up and out of himself in a sheet of flame; it comes to the soldier, war-mad on a stricken

field and refusing quarter; and it came to Buck, leading the pack, sounding the old wolf cry. . . .

A thematic epitome, perhaps. But the passage contradicts even
London's own thought. His art, usually so didactic in nature,
rarely displays forgetfulness of purpose, but is instead pain-
fully aware of the condition of being alive. And although in his
essay "The Yellow Peril," London claims, "War is to-day the
final arbiter in the affairs of men, and it is as yet the final test
of the worthwhileness of peoples," in the October 1913 issue
of the *International Socialist Review*, London writes, "Young
men: The lowest aim in your life is to become a soldier." The
passage Labor cites may indeed be a "thematic epitome" of
The Call of the Wild, but as well it illustrates that London's
ideas, which never seem to fuse into a single philosophy, find
their resolution only in a creature that is not human. We human beings have no chance of being the ideal hero which is
Buck. We must forever remain befuddled and confused by the
tension between that which is animalistic and warlike in us
and that which is social and moral.

Mr. Labor's concluding remarks about *The Call of the
Wild* contradict his earlier thesis that the book is a "Myth
of the Hero." A hero is, if nothing else, a moral construct.
As a moral construct, a hero is, by definition, didactic. Labor
writes in "Jack London's *Mondo Cane*":

> *The Call of the Wild* . . . is purely aesthetic and intransi-
> tive, engaging the reader in a rapt attention for no other
> purpose than the unique experience of art. Rather than
> stressing "the marvelous power and influence of environ-
> ment," *The Call of the Wild* stresses more subtly something
> marvelous within man, the miracle of the "artistic transac-
> tion" and, ultimately, the eternal mystery of life itself. For
> this reason it retains its stature as a great world classic.

Mr. Labor's sentiments seem sincere and are certainly enthusiastic concerning Jack London. They are touching and seem to come from his heart. His heart aside, however, for the premier Jack London scholar to assert that anything London writes is "purely aesthetic and intransitive" makes this reader, at least, think that Mr. Labor, in the fever of the critical moment, is telling some stretchers for the sake of his argument. The novel's chapter headings alone—"Into the Primitive," "The Law of Club and Fang," "The Dominant Primordial Beast," "Who Has Won to Mastership," "The Toil of Trace and Trail," "For the Love of a Man," and "The Sounding of the Call"—sound like the titles of Socialist propaganda tracts or chapter headings from Nietzsche.

London believes we are flawed beasts, that, as he writes in "The Somnambulists," any of us is "the same man that once drank blood from his enemy's skull," that we are animals—flawed animals which, because of the pittance of morality we have shackled ourselves with, can never attain freedom. Buck, London's famous dog, attains the freedom we can never have. The interesting problem created by the book's didacticism is that London teaches a lesson that is impossible to learn. There is no going back. We can only live in a state of rueful social and moral contradiction. It is a lesson we either don't want to learn or one that, if we wanted to learn it, would be impossible to learn. The lesson London preaches is utterly impracticable. The greatness of *The Call of the Wild* rests not in its "pure" aesthetics, but in its *confused* aesthetics, its ideology of The Ideal.

Notes

¹ It is worth citing a long passage from *The Sea Wolf* here. Wolf Larsen, the Ahab-like dictator of his boat, spouts on endlessly in the novel concerning his Darwinian/Nietzschean philosophy. The following passage is typical (Wolf Larsen begins the conversation):

> "I believe that life is a mess," he answered promptly. "It is like yeast, a ferment, a thing that moves and may move for a minute, an hour, a year, or a hundred years, but that in the end will cease to move. The big eat the little that they may continue to move, the strong eat the weak that they may retain their strength. The lucky eat the most amd move the longest, that is all."
>
> He swept his arm in an impatient gesture toward a number of the sailors who were working on some kind of rope stuff amidships.
>
> "They move; so does the jellyfish move. They move in order to eat in order that they may keep moving. There you have it. They live for their belly's sake, and the belly is for their sake. It's a circle; you get nowhere. Neither do they. In the end they come to a standstill. They move no more. They are dead."
>
> "They have dreams," I interrupted, "radiant, flashing dreams—"
>
> "Of grub," he concluded sententiously.
>
> "And of more—"
>
> "Grub. Of a larger appetite and more luck in satisfying it." His voice sounded harsh. There was no levity in it. "For look you, they dream of making lucky voyages which will bring them more money, of becoming the mates of ships, of finding fortunes—in short, of being in a better position for preying on their fellows, of having all night in, good grub, and somebody else

to do the dirty work. You and I are just like them. There is no difference, except that we have eaten more and better. I am eating them now, and you, too. But in the past you have eaten more than I have. You have slept in soft beds, and worn fine clothes, and eaten good meals. Who made those beds? and those clothes? and those meals? Not you. You never made anything in your own sweat. You live on an income which your father earned. You are like a frigate bird swooping down upon the boobies and robbing them of the fish they have caught. You are one with a crowd of men who have made what they call a government, who are masters of all the other men, and who eat the food the other men get and would like to eat themselves. You wear the warm clothes. They made the clothes, but they shiver in rags and ask you, the lawyer, or business agent who handles your money, for a job."

"But that is beside the matter," I cried.

"Not at all." He was speaking rapidly, now, and his eyes were flashing. "It is piggishness, and it is life. Of what use or sense is an immortality of piggishness? What is the end? What is it all about? You have made no food. Yet the food you have eaten or wasted might have saved the lives of a score of wretches who made the food but did not eat it. What immortal end did you serve? Or did they? Consider yourself and me. What does your boasted immortality amount to when your life runs foul of mine? You would like to go back to the land, which is a favorable place for your kind of pig-gishness. It is a whim of mine to keep you aboard this ship, where my piggishness flourishes. And keep you I will. I may make or break you. You may die to-day, this week, or next month. I could kill you now, with a blow of my fist, for you are a miserable weakling. But if we are immortal, what is the reason for this? To be pig-gish as you and I have been all our lives does not seem to be just the thing for immortals to be doing. Again, what's it all about? Why have I kept you here?—"

"Because you are stronger," I managed to blurt out.

"But why stronger?" he went on at once with his perpetual queries. "Because I am a bigger bit of the ferment than you? Don't you see? Don't you see?"

"But the hopelessness of it," I protested.

"I agree with you," he answered. "Then why move at all, since moving is living? Without moving and being part of the yeast there would be no hopelessness. But,— and there it is,—we want to live and move, though we have no reason to, because it happens that it is the nature of life to live and move, to want to live and move. If it were not for this, life would be dead. It is because of this life that is in you that you dream of your immortality. The life that is in you is alive and wants to go on being alive forever. Bah! An eternity of piggishness!"

[2] The strike London appears to be writing about in "South of the Slot" is described in Robert Glass Cleland's *California in Our Time* as follows:

> The struggle between capital and labor organizations reached a climax during the summer of 1901 when the powerful Employers' Association, uncompromisingly hostile to organized labor, determined to break the unions' control in San Francisco and engaged in a war to the finish with the combination of waterfront unions known as the City Front Federation. The ensuing struggle degenerated into a brutal knock-down, drag-out, dog-eat-dog affair in which both labor and capital sought to destroy each other, regardless of the effect of the conflict upon either themselves or the community at large.
>
> As the strike spread, business in San Francisco, as well as in many other parts of northern California, was

brought to a standstill, and the resultant loss amounted
to nearly a million dollars a day. The wholesale acts of
intimidation and violence to which both sides resorted
led to the death of five men and the injury of several
hundred others. In the end the Employers' Associa-
tion broke the strike and successfully maintained the
principle of the open shop for its members. This result
was achieved primarily by the use of a huge war chest
and Mayor Phelan's active suppression of violence by
means of the San Francisco police.

[3] London's essay "The Tramp" offers much on the subject.
London argues that the Tramp is a logical by-product of the
capitalist system of society, and should be understood as such.
He writes:

> But the tramp does not usually come from the slums.
> His place of birth is ordinarily a bit above, and some-
> times a very great bit above. A confessed failure, he yet
> refuses to accept the punishment, and swerves aside
> from the slum to vagabondage. The average beast
> in the social pit is either too much of a beast, or too
> much of a slave to the bourgeois ethics and ideals of
> his masters, to manifest this flicker or rebellion. But
> the social pit, out of its discouragement and vicious-
> ness, breeds criminals, men who prefer being beasts
> of prey to being beasts of work. And the mediocre
> criminal, in turn, the unfit and inefficient criminal,
> is discouraged by the strong arm of the law and goes
> over to trampdom.
>
> These men, the discouraged worker and the dis-
> couraged criminal, voluntarily withdraw themselves
> from the struggle for work. Industry does not need
> them. There are no factories shut down through lack
> of labor, no projected railroads unbuilt for want of
> pick-and-shovel men. Women are still glad to toil for

a dollar a week, and men and boys to clamor and fight for work at the factory gates. No one misses these discouraged men, and in going away they have made it somewhat easier for those that remain.

[4] The complaint lodged against London appears in the *New York Call* of March 27, 1916. A portion of it, as quoted by Philip S. Foner, reads as follows:

> We can assure him [London] that, however tediously peaceable membership in Glen Ellen may be, the workingmen in mine and shop and factory who make up the rank and file of the Socialist Party are fighting—not always an exhilarating, romantic, spectacular fight—not always the sort of fight that makes good copy for the magazines or good films for the movies—but the steady, unflinching, uncomplaining, unboasting, shoulder to shoulder and inch-by-inch fight that uses the fighters up one by one and sends them to the soon-forgotten graves, but that gains ground for those who fill up the ranks as they fall, that undermines the enemy's defenses and wears him down and keeps on wearing him down until the time comes for breaking his line and making the grand dash that shall end the war.

XI

CONCLUSION

Our notions of what constitutes "literature" in America are problematic today.

The canon is under fire as increasingly people from humble beginnings are entering the academy and becoming writers.

Working-class academics are bringing their values and their conflicts with them to the classroom, to their editorial duties, to their aesthetic stances in the articles they publish, in the anthologies they edit.

Working-class writers are repudiating the values and aesthetic criteria of the two-millennia-strong aristocratic stronghold over Letters.

The Greeks wrote about gods and royalty. The Christians wrote about their God and His worshippers. The European aristocracies recruited talent to sing their praises and promote their aesthetic ideals. The Americans—degenerate Europeans—aped the Europeans.

But now Europe is a colony of America, and soon it will be a colony of Asia. Its aristocracies are all but gone, and plutocracies are sprouting like Hydra's heads. As spring plutocracies, so spring artists with blood that's not blue.

The European tradition of excellence in Art will endure. Alongside it, however, rises a particularly 20th-century notion of Art. The canon is opening up.

Toni Morrison doesn't hold a candle to Günter Grass and Carlos Fuentes aesthetically. Comparing her prose to theirs is like comparing Dreiser's to that of Henry James. But Morrison has a Nobel Prize. Fuentes doesn't.

Heinold's First and Last Chance Saloon, the bar on the Oakland waterfront where Jack London did much of his early boozing, has been named a historical literary landmark by Friends of the Library USA, right alongside the Algonquin Hotel and Poe's home in Philadelphia. The National Trust for Historic Preservation is working on turning Cannery Row in John Steinbeck's Monterey into a National Historic Site.

London and Steinbeck and Toni Morrison aren't writing stuff that Walter Pater would consider Art. But it's plain that Walter Pater's take on things is losing its authority.

The work of writers whose notions of aesthetics differ from the traditional notions is being reassessed, and this reassessment will continue. It will unearth writers whose work is truly atrocious, as is some of Jack London's worst. It will unearth work which might better have been left buried. But it will also unearth some gold, some work that has long been neglected and that can help breed a new generation of writers, a generation that will have more options than merely further refining Art beyond the limits of common human understanding, a generation of writers that will not have to bow their heads in reverence to the wealthy keepers of the gate.

Jack London hates the rich, even after he's become one of them. And he hates the poor, too. Hates them with a passion that is nearly unparalleled, that is pathological. He'd prefer either a society of animals in which we all fought it out, or a Socialist society in which we all worked and we all divvied up the goods equally. Either would be more fair than Capitalism. If it were brawn, he'd survive the fisticuffs, and if it were Socialist, everyone would survive.

It's no contradiction. It's the story of any poor boy done good. It's the story of a black Republican. It's the story of a trailer-trash Okie who finds oil on his property. It's the story of any worker who rises out of the lower classes and into the moneyed classes.

The problem London is trying to work out is not an eccentric one: it's merely a problem that hasn't been often presented. People from the working classes only in the past hundred years in America have gained the minimum education necessary to be able to pen their visions of the world. People in the working classes have historically been underrepresented in literature because they neither read nor wrote it. Now they still don't, for the most part, read literature. But sometimes, and with increasing frequency, they are climbing the ladder out of the sewer and poking their heads through the manhole and seeing what lives above ground. In 20th-century America the poor have begun to make the leap to financial security, a prerequisite for the creation of Art, and the poor who make the leap find themselves faced with London's dilemma.

The reason literature isn't full of examples of London's seeming contradictory views is that the poor haven't had the inclination or capacity to voice their views. They're beginning to get both. And we'll be hearing more of London's dilemma.

Just a few years ago, the pop music star Queen Latifah drove her Mercedes-Benz into Harlem as a gesture of camaraderie. The local citizens carjacked her Mercedes and performed the robbery with the customary physical violence. I'm sure her feelings about the citizens of Harlem are slightly ambiguous. If they weren't before she crossed 110th Street, they most likely are now.

When London is writing a book like *The People of the Abyss* or a short story like "South of the Slot," a book which ostensibly has compassion for the ghetto-dwellers or a short story which lauds the working man and condemns the Capitalist oppressors, he genuinely has compassion for the poor, he genuinely wishes they had a Socialist government which saw to it that they weren't being worked to death and made beasts. He sees them, and it's like looking in a mirror.

But he's not kidding himself. In that mirror there is a crowd, and in that crowd, there is one in a million that isn't a beast irrevocably, that isn't deserving of their station in life. It's hard for him to say what he really thinks: that he is superior to them, that he is more deserving of escape because he is not a weakling or a stupid person.

So sometimes he says it in his fiction. He says it when he glorifies Nietzschean Supermen. When he creates a character like Wolf Larsen or the Malemute Kid, he's saying, basically, "Some humans are better than others."

Neither of these two options works. Not even for London.

So he creates Buck. He creates a beast that is superior to the other beasts, that is free to be the beast it is without incurring the moral disdain of its fellow beasts. He writes *The Call of the Wild* and presents a character that is the perfection of being, a character that is noble not by human standards, but by all the harsh logic, the white logic of the North.

The sadness of London's work as a whole is that he cannot figure out a way to present Buck as a human option.

Would Buck were human.

Would we were beast.

BIBLIOGRAPHY

Achebe, Chinua. "An Image of Africa: Conrad's *Heart of Darkness.*" *The Story and its Writer: An Introduction to Short Fiction*. Ann Charters ed. 4th ed. Boston: Bedford Books, 1995.

Auerbach, Jonathan. "Congested Mails: Buck and Jack's 'Call.'" *Rereading Jack London*. Leonard Cassuto and Jeanne Campbell Reesman, eds. Stanford: Stanford UP, 1996.

_____. *Male Call: Becoming Jack London*. Durham: Duke UP, 1996.

Bamford, Georgia Loring. *The Mystery of Jack London: Some of His Friends, Also a Few Letters: A Reminiscence*. Folcroft, PA: The Folcroft Press, 1931.

Barltrop, Robert. *Jack London: the Man, the Writer, the Rebel*. London: Pluto Press, 1976.

Barthelme, Donald. "Not-Knowing." *Not-Knowing: The Essays and Interviews*. New York: Random House, 1997.

_____. "On the Level of Desire: Catalog Introduction for an Exhibition of Work by Sherrie Levine, Mary Boone/Michael Werner Gallery, New York, 1987." *Not-Knowing: The Essays and Interviews*. New York: Random House, 1997.

Berrigan, Ted. *So Going Around Cities: New & Selected Poems 1958–1979*. Berkeley: Blue Wind Press, 1980.

Blake, William. *The Marriage of Heaven and Hell. The Norton Anthology of English Literature*. Vol. 2. 6th ed. M. H. Abrams, ed. New York: Norton, 1993.

Blewer, James L. "The Griswold Effect." *Southern Plains Review*. 1:1 (Spring) 1991.

Bloom, Harold. *The Anxiety of Influence: A Theory of Poetry*. London: Oxford UP, 1973.

_____. *The Western Canon*. New York: Harcourt Brace, 1994.

Brodhead, Richard. *Cultures of Letters*. Chicago: U of Chicago P, 1993.

Camus, Albert. *Notebooks: 1942–1951*. New York: Knopf, 1965.

Cassuto, Leonard and Jeanne Campbell Reesman. "Introduction: Jack London, a Representative Man." *Rereading Jack London*. Stanford: Stanford UP, 1996.

Chow, Willard T. *The Reemergence of an Inner City: The Pivot of Chinese Settlement in the East Bay Region of the San Francisco Bay Area*. San Francisco: R&E Research Associates, 1977.

Cioran, E. M. *Drawn and Quartered*. Richard Howard tr. New York: Seaver Books, 1983.

Cleland, Robert Glass. *California in Our Time: 1900–1940*. New York: Knopf, 1947.

Conrad, Joseph. *Heart of Darkness. The Norton Anthology of English Literature*. Vol. 2. 6th ed. Ed. Meyer Abrams et al. New York: Norton, 1993.

———. "Preface to *The Nigger of the 'Narcissus'*." *The Norton Anthology of English Literature*. Vol. 2. 6th ed. Ed. Meyer Abrams et al. New York: Norton, 1993.

Crane, Stephen. "The Open Boat." *Great Short Works of Stephen Crane*. New York: Harper & Row, 1968.

Derrick, Scott. "Making a Heterosexual Man: Gender, Sexuality, and Narrative in the Fiction of Jack London." *Rereading Jack London*. Leonard Cassuto and Jeanne Campbell Reesman, eds. Stanford: Stanford UP, 1996.

Emerson, Ralph Waldo. "The American Scholar." *Selected Writings of Emerson*. New York: Modern Library, 1981.

———. "Self-Reliance." *Selected Writings of Emerson*. New York: Modern Library, 1981.

Faulkner, William. *New York Times Book Review*. January 30, 1955.

Feied, Frederick. *No Pie in the Sky: The Hobo as American Cultural Hero in the Works of Jack London, John Dos Passos, and Jack Kerouac*. New York: The Citadel Press, 1964.

Foner, Philip S. *Jack London: American Rebel*. New York: Citadel, 1947.

Johnston, Carolyn. *Jack London—An American Radical?* Westport, CT: Greenwood P, 1984.

Johnson, Marilynn S. *The Second Gold Rush: Oakland and the East Bay in World War II*. Berkeley: U of California P, 1993.

Kershaw, Alex. *Jack London: A Life*. New York: St. Martin's, 1998.

Labor, Earle. "Introduction." *The Complete Short Stories of Jack London*. 3 vols. Ed. Earle Labor et al. Stanford: Stanford UP, 1993.

_____. *Jack London*. New York: Twayne, 1994.

_____. "Jack London's *Mondo Cane*: 'Bâtard,' *The Call of the Wild* and *White Fang*." *Critical Essays on Jack London*. Ed. Jacqueline Tavernier-Courbain. Boston: G. K. Hall, 1983.

Lawrence, D. H. "Americans." *D. H. Lawrence: Selected Literary Criticism*. Ed. Anthony Beal. New York: Viking, 1966.

_____. "Autobiographical Sketch." *D. H. Lawrence: Selected Literary Criticism*. Ed. Anthony Beal. New York: Viking, 1966.

_____. "Bottom Dogs." *D. H. Lawrence: Selected Literary Criticism*. Ed. Anthony Beal. New York: Viking, 1966.

_____. *Studies in Classic American Literature*. New York: Viking, 1966.

London, Charmian. *The Book of Jack London*. 2 vols. New York: The Century Co., 1921.

London, Jack. *Before Adam*. New York: Ace Books, 1906.

_____. *The Call of the Wild. The Works of Jack London*. Ed. Paul J. Horowitz. New York: Avenal Books, 1980.

_____. "The Class Struggle." *War of the Classes*. New York: The Regent Press, 1905.

_____. *The Complete Short Stories of Jack London*. Ed. Earle Labor et. al. 3 vols. Stanford: Stanford UP, 1993.

_____. "Getting into Print." *The Portable Jack London*. Ed. Earle Labor. New York: Penguin, 1994.

_____. *The Iron Heel. Jack London: Novels and Social Writings*. New York: Library of America, 1982.

_____. *The Letters of Jack London*. Ed. Earle Labor et al. 3 vols. Stanford: Stanford UP, 1988.

_____. "The Other Animals." *Revolution and Other Essays*. New York: The Macmillan Company, 1912.

_____. *The People of the Abyss. Jack London: Novels and Social Writings*. New York: Library of America, 1982.

_____. "The Question of the Maximum." *War of the Classes*. New York: The Regent Press, 1905.

_____. *The Sea Wolf*. New York: Grosset & Dunlap, 1904.

_____. "The Somnambulists." *Revolution and Other Essays*. New York: The Macmillan Company, 1912

_____. *The Star Rover*. London: Alan Sutton Publishing Limited, 1986.

_____. "The Terrible and Tragic in Fiction." *The Jack London Reports: War Correspondence, Sports Articles, and Miscellaneous Writings*. Ed.

King Hendricks and Irving Shepherd. Garden City, NY: Doubleday, 1970.

_____. "These Bones Shall Rise Again." *Revolution and Other Essays*. New York: The Macmillan Company, 1912.

_____. "The Tramp." *War of the Classes*. New York: The Regent Press, 1905.

_____. *The Valley of the Moon*. New York: Macmillan, 1911.

_____. *War of the Classes*. New York: The Regent Press, 1905.

_____. "What Life Means to Me." *Revolution and Other Essays*. New York: The Macmillan Company, 1912.

_____. *White Fang*. New York: Macmillan, 1906.

_____. "The Yellow Peril." *Revolution and Other Essays*. New York: The Macmillan Company, 1912.

London, Joan. *Jack London and His Times: An Unconventional Biography*. New York: Doubleday, Doran & Co., 1939.

Lundquist, James. *Jack London: Adventures, Ideas, and Fiction*. New York: Ungar, 1987.

Mencken, H. L. "Jack London." *Prejudices, First Series*. New York: Knopf, 1919.

McClintock, James I. *Jack London's Strong Truths*. East Lansing: Michigan State University P, 1997.

Mills, Gordon. "The Transformation of Material in a Mimetic Fiction." *Jack London: Essays in Criticism*. Santa Barbara: Peregrine Smith, 1978.

Mowry, George E. *The California Progressives*. Berkeley: U of California P, 1951.

Nabokov, Vladimir. *Strong Opinions*. New York: McGraw-Hill, 1973.

Nietzsche, Friedrich. *Twilight of the Idols*. R. J. Hollingdale tr. New York: Penguin, 1990.

_____. *The Wanderer and His Shadow. Basic Writings of Nietzsche*. Walter Kaufmann tr. New York: Modern Library, 1968.

O'Connor, Richard. *Jack London: A Biography*. Boston: Little, Brown and Company, 1964.

O'Rourke, P. J. *Parliament of Whores: A Lone Humorist Attempts to Explain the Entire U.S. Government*. New York: Vintage, 1992.

Ownbey, Ray Wilson. "Introduction: London in the Seventies." *Jack London: Essays in Criticism*. Santa Barbara: Peregrine Smith, 1978.

Pater, Walter. "'Conclusion' to The Renaissance." *The Norton Anthology of English Literature*. Vol. 2. 6th ed. Ed. Meyer Abrams et al. New York: Norton, 1993

Peluso, Robert. "Gazing at Royalty: Jack London's 'The People of the Abyss' and the Emergence of American Imperialism." *Rereading Jack London*. Leonard Cassuto and Jeanne Campbell Reesman, eds. Stanford: Stanford UP, 1996.

Perry, John. *Jack London: An American Myth*. Chicago: Nelson-Hall, 1981.

Schopenhauer, Arthur. "On Books and Writing." *Essays and Aphorisms*. R. J. Hollingdale tr. New York: Penguin, 1970.

Schor, Francis. "Power, Gender, and Ideological Discourse in *The Iron Heel*." *Rereading Jack London*. Leonard Cassuto and Jeanne Campbell Reesman, eds. Stanford: Stanford UP, 1996.

Sinclair, Upton. *Letters to Judd, An American Workingman*. Pamphlet. 1925.

Spinner, Jonathan Harold. "Jack London's *Martin Eden*: The Development of the Existential Hero." *Jack London: Essays in Criticism*. Santa Barbara: Peregrine Smith, 1978.

Stasz, Clarice. "Social Darwinism, Gender, and Humor in 'Adventure.'" *Rereading Jack London*. Leonard Cassuto and Jeanne Campbell Reesman, eds. Stanford: Stanford UP, 1996.

Stone, Irving. *Sailor on Horseback: The Biography of Jack London*. Cambridge, MA: Houghton Mifflin, 1938.

Swift, Jonathan. *Gulliver's Travels. Gulliver's Travels and Other Writings*. Ed. Louis A. Landa. Boston: Houghton Mifflin, 1960.

Tavernier-Courbin, Jacqueline. "Jack London: A Professional." *Critical Essays on Jack London*. Ed. Jacqueline Tavernier-Courbain. Boston: G.K. Hall, 1983.

Trilling, Lionel. *The Liberal Imagination*. Garden City: Doubleday, 1953.

Tuttleton, James. "Some Modern Sophists." *Vital Signs: Essays on American Literature and Criticism*. Chicago: Ivan R. Dee, 1996.

Whitman, Walt. *Song of Myself. Anthology of American Literature, Volume I: Colonial through Romantic*. George McMichael et al. eds. Upper Saddle River, N.J.: Prentice Hall, 1997.

Wilde, Oscar. "Phrases and Philosophies for the Use of the Young." *Aesthetes and Decadents*. Revised Edition. Karl Beckson ed. Chicago: Academy, 1981.

Williams, James. "Commitment and Practice: The Authorship of Jack London" *Rereading Jack London*. Leonard Cassuto and Jeanne Campbell Reesman, eds. Stanford: Stanford UP, 1996.

INDEX

Eric Miles Williamson is the author of two novels, *East Bay Grease* and *Two-Up*. A PEN/Hemingway finalist and winner of an NEA Fellowship for fiction as well as a Christopher Isherwood fellowship, he edits *American Book Review* and is on the Board of Directors of the National Book Critics Circle. He lives on the Texas/Mexico border, sixty miles from the mouth of the Rio Grande, with his wife, Judy, and their sons, Guthrie and Turner.